Between TWO Tigers

D0109751

Testimonies
of
Vietnamese
Christians

Compiled by Tom White

Between Two Tigers

Published by Living Sacrifice Book Company, a division of The Voice of the Martyrs, P.O. Box 2273, Bartlesville, OK 74005-2273.

First Printing 1996

Cover illustration by Nancy Harkins
Design and typesetting by Genesis Publications
Sketches by Grace Kim

Scripture quotations are taken from the New King James version, ©1979, 1980, 1982 by Thomas Nelson Inc., Publishers, Nashville, Tennessee.

Library of Congress Cataloging-in-Publication Data
Between two tigers : testimonies of Vietnamese Christians /
   compiled by Tom White.
       p.   cm.
   ISBN 0-88264-322-3
   1. Persecution—Vietnam—Biography.   2. Evangelistic work—
Vietnam—History—20th century.   3. Persecution—Vietnam—
History—20th century.   4. Vietnam—Church history—20th
century.   [1. Bible—Publication and distribution—Vietnam.]
I. White, Tom, 1947-   .
BR1608.5.B47   1996
275.97'0825'0922—dc20
   [B]   96-32072
                                                    CIP

Table of Contents

Dedication

THIS BOOK is dedicated to my children, Dorothy and Daniel, and to my grandchildren, with the hope that they live in the flow of God's love and purpose not by trying to wash their own clean feet again and again, but by washing the feet of the world.

Don Tanner, an editor of my past books, went to be with the Lord in the midst of his work on this book. A gentle, literary presence on the staff of Campus Crusade for Christ, Don now rejoices with many of those whose lives have been changed by his gospel endeavors.

Foreword

≜

S INCE 1947 when Pastor Richard Wurmbrand, the foun-
der of our organization, The Voice of the Martyrs, began
working with Christians from captive nations, there has been
no "denominational prejudice" when giving Scriptures or
financial help to those who were persecuted. We have helped
Baptists in Russia, Catholics in Albania, Pentecostals in Vietnam, many in areas where there was no one else to mention
the forbidden name of Jesus.

The Christian witnesses in this book come from many
denominational backgrounds. Their boldness to stand up in
the face of adversity, distribute Bibles, and proclaim Christ
outweighs any denominational "difference."

We all have been caught in our comfortable denominational armchairs pointing doctrinal fingers at each other
through the doors of our open church buildings on "every
corner." We have gathered on councils seeking areas of agreement, but simple agreement on particular doctrine is not
obeying God. Agreement requires no energy. Agreement does
not produce new converts to Christ. The Christians who dare
to illegally baptize in the jungles of Vietnam, or who return to
worship on the ashes of hundreds of churches burned by
Muslims in Africa, understand the priorities. Jesus' blood
purchased us to propagate the kingdom of God. The Great
Commandment was not about doctrinal agreement (which is
a base), but about the act of loving God and the act of loving
your neighbor.

Christians around the world receive their orders and are
obedient to Him. From our sheltered environment we are all
too eager to poke in and tell them how to witness. Or we sit

back and criticize the different doctrines of those reaching out for Christ and yet do not reach out ourselves.

Although our Statement of Faith reflects an evangelical stand, we once delivered eight Bibles to a Catholic priest in Central Vietnam. He had not seen a Bible for 20 years. He joyfully received them to give to others in the countryside. If someone who had no money for a Bible—and who was not allowed by their government to own a Bible—reached out their hand and asked you for one, what would you do? In the 60 seconds of this dangerous opportunity, would you ask them for a doctrinal statement or hand them the Bread of Life?

Such is the hunger in Vietnam. In Communist Vietnam there are government-monitored official churches, Catholic and Protestant, and four major unofficial or "underground" house church movements. There are Baptists, Pentecostals, and others. Christians have been persecuted in Vietnam for 300 years. Non-Christian religions in Vietnam do not experience the same level of persecution as the Christians experience, since Buddhists and animists do not represent a great threat to the Communists. The Great Commission of Christ's love is a spiritual threat to the powers of darkness.

Some provinces in Vietnam control the church and imprison pastors much more readily than other areas. In North Vietnam, the Hanoi government allows only about ten official church buildings to remain open although the Christian population multiplies rapidly, numbering in the hundreds of thousands. Nowhere in Vietnam is permission given to construct new church buildings.

Although the government of Vietnam has allowed the printing of limited quantities of Bibles, some of the Christians who give their testimonies in this book are now sitting in prison for distributing those Bibles. The Vietnamese government still does not allow the printing or importation of any Christian literature in the languages of the more than 60 tribes encompassing over six million souls. Although they are

Vietnamese citizens, these tribes speak different languages
and have different racial backgrounds.

I am thankful to the humble Christians of Vietnam whom
I have met and others like them. They show my family that we
are spiritually enriched and called to live a holy life in our
wealthy countries for a purpose. Eternal joy still hides under
the unattractive cloak of sacrifice and commitment. Some of
the tribal evangelists I meet do not know how to open a can of
Coca-Cola but have brought their entire village to Christ. I
know how to open the can. Can I open a heart? Those whom
I have met illustrate the little-mentioned church of 2 Corin-
thians 6:10, "as having nothing and yet possessing all things."
They remind me that the most permanent blessing comes
from giving that blessing to others with no thought of keeping
it and consuming it upon myself.

You may not agree with portions of the shining Vietnamese
testimonies in this book. Total agreement is not necessary. It
is my prayer that at least you will be inspired by the holy
boldness and simplicity of these Vietnamese Christians as they
seek to obey Christ's commandment to go into *all* the world.
May we do likewise.

> Tom White
> USA Director
> The Voice of the Martyrs

The Burning Message

THE VIETNAMESE have a saying, "If you use a blanket to cover yourself, then you will know whether or not there are lice inside that blanket." Many people who live outside Vietnam have reported that the people have freedom of religion. But if you really want to find out the truth about their way of life, live for a few weeks inside their country and walk in the shoes of the members of the persecuted church.

The trials these Christian brothers and sisters experience are heart-rending. Every day pastors are arrested, children are left without their parents, families live in poverty—all for the sake of Christ.

The church in Vietnam was born and raised in adversity. From the first moment, those who claimed the name of Christ have suffered in many forms. The Christians live between two "tigers"—Communism and Buddhism/tribal religions. No matter which way they turn, they face a tiger threatening them. In the tribal villages, in the cities, in the countryside, informers and those who oppose the gospel lay in wait to sabotage their faith.

But the Christians in Vietnam do not stop because of their imminent danger. Instead, they travel lonely roads to remote villages, face police interrogation and prison, all with a sense of joy and accomplishment in Christ's power.

How Did It All Begin?

Vietnam is a small country in Indochina that has suffered greatly. The nation has been wounded from head to toe by various wars. As a result, the people became bitter and felt as if their lives were being sacrificed to the philosophy of Communism. Seeking deliverance, they swam in a sea of sin.

At the same time, Buddhism was brought in from China. Soon every town and village had pagodas, shrines, and temples. Idols adorned every home, and all classes of people celebrated superstitious religious rites.

The Church in the North

These changes did not help the church. Communism, its greatest source of persecution, began around 1954 and still continues. The government began to confiscate church buildings and threaten those who claimed to be Catholic or Protestant. Officials considered Christians to be anti-country, anti-government, and unpatriotic.

The oppression was more severe in the North than in the South. After Vietnam was divided into two parts, 100,000 Catholics and Protestants escaped from the North and settled in the South. The Christians who remained had their property confiscated and many were imprisoned. The officials destroyed Bibles and tore down all the crosses. Newspapers and broadcasting companies spread false in-

Decades later, 292 churches remain closed by the Communists. This closed church's cross was broken off and replaced with a Communist star.

formation about believers, while atheism and Darwinism were taught. The persecution of the North Vietnamese church became so severe that today the people in many large cities know nothing about the gospel and have never heard the name of Jesus or even seen a Bible.

One way the government succeeded in dimming the light of the church was by controlling the activities of church leaders. Since 1954, the Christian Missionary Alliance (CMA) in the North has not been allowed to preach freely, and pastors are forced to study politics. Therefore, many have turned away from the true way.

For example, Pastor Bui, vice chairman of the CMA church, is a policeman within the official church and is considered a spy by the Christians. From his North Vietnamese headquarters, he endorses Communism and boldly announces his beliefs from the pulpit.

Bibles are printed only in small quantities while Christians are growing by the tens of thousands. Bibles printed in the South are not allowed in the North where there are over 100,000 H'mong tribesmen who are new converts. We trust in God's people around the world to help fill that need, one way or another.

Delivering the Burning Message

The hearts of the North Vietnamese people are tender. They are like a tree in the desert that needs water to live. They are like soldiers defeated in the battlefields, now embracing the gospel.

Why are the people so open to the gospel? They have lost their way in the maze of human philosophy. The idealism of Communism that they pursued for so long collapsed before their eyes. Like the prodigal son, today many throw away everything to respond to the call from heaven.

In every province, Christians are preaching the gospel. But the number of disciples working in God's fields is very small.

Their efforts are like salt thrown into the ocean. The task is so huge and the work is still limited.

Who is willing to go to these people? Of the thousands of Vietnamese who moved to the South after 1975 are a few who believed in the Lord Jesus and have returned to their home areas that have no witness. Some North Vietnamese have come back from refugee camps in Hong Kong to spread the gospel. Others have heard the good news through Far East Broadcasting Company radio broadcasts from Manila and have received the Lord.

The number who believe in Jesus increases every day. They meet in houses and worship the Lord at home. They are threatened and punished by the local government officials, and their names and addresses are announced on TV and over the radio to warn others of them.

The Harvest Field

The lack of funds limits the work in Vietnam. Although there are official churches in the large cities, many Christians do not join because the pastors are controlled by the government. In these pulpits, the complete Word of God cannot be shared. The second coming of Christ cannot be mentioned.

Therefore, these Christians have formed house churches. Most groups contain ten to twelve people who have continued meeting for months, even years. While the members learn and practice their faith in small churches, they also care for their families and new converts. The pastors teach the right point of view from the living Word of God. Because of this, they endure persecution from the government and from official church leaders who work with government leaders.

When the church in the South began bringing the "burning" message of the gospel to the North, fires of revival began to lift the hearts of many Christians. This has given these saints a deep desire to reach out to others. Previously, no one dared to bring the gospel to the tribal people because they were afraid that the government would accuse them of joining hands with the Phu Ko (a tribal anti-government movement). But now, the revival has sent believers to the tribal areas. The church has become a great army with a banner lifted high, marching with tears pouring down in joy as recorded in Ezekiel 37:9,10, explaining how the Spirit of the Lord Jehovah is visiting His people:

> Then He said to me, "Prophesy to the breath, prophesy, son of man, and say to the breath, 'Thus says the Lord God: "Come from the four winds, O breath, and breathe on these slain, that they may live." ' " So I prophesied as He commanded me, and breath came into them, and they lived, and stood upon their feet, an exceedingly great army.

Rooted in a Dry Land

Today, Vietnam is truly a ripe field waiting to be harvested. Amid the persecution and beatings, Communist Party members are becoming witnesses for Christ among their colleagues. Who could have predicted that in the land of Communism, party members would preach Christ's message to their comrades? The church is rising up, like a root growing deep in a dry land, strong under fiery trials, claiming Christ's resurrected power so the gates of hell will not prevail against it.

Jesus Christ is changing the course of history in Vietnam. The church has been established and many lives are wholeheartedly dedicated to Christ. The gospel is being preached all over the land, to many tribes, up to the time when the end will come.

In this book, you will hear the words of those who are in the midst of the harvest. Their stories are presented so that you can pray for them and use *their* testimonies to boldly proclaim the burning message in your corner of the world.

CHAPTER 1

In the Midst
of Persecution

❧

An Open Door

The police began to secretly follow me to my school to investigate what I was doing. One Communist Party member in the school told a Christian teacher why they were there, then this teacher told me. Two days later, two policemen came to my home and questioned my children.

In Vietnam, people are not allowed to share their faith outside of the church building. Christians keep silent and try to find a way to serve the Lord. They pray together and worship the Lord in homes. But sometimes the police still find out.

The afternoon that the policemen came and asked for me, my 17-year-old son, Do Huy Du, answered the door. He realized they were police because one man

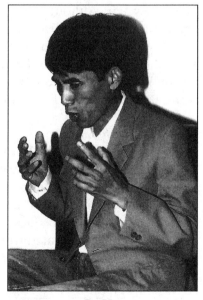

Do Huy

1

wore civilian clothes and the other man wore a police uniform. He told them I was not at home.

They asked, "Do you have meetings in your home regularly? Do any preachers come to your home?"

My son answered, "In my home we pray regularly. We go to church regularly to meet. Because my dad is a teacher, many other teachers come."

When I returned home from work, I met the two policemen waiting for me in front of my house. I invited them to come in.

They said, "We know that you follow this Tin Lanh[1] (Protestant) religion. Tell us what you know about the Tin Lanh religion."

I shared the gospel with them and gave a testimony of how the Lord dealt with my life. Whenever I openly mentioned any name, they very carefully questioned me in detail about that person. I naively mentioned people in the official church and also in the underground church. When it got dark an hour later, they left. Although they said they would come back again, they did not return.

I later learned that these policemen were Tien and Van from the city's PA Sixteen Security Police office. The police station has many branches; some are in charge of economics, some are over politics. PA Sixteen is in charge of religion.

Encounter with Christ

Before I came to know the Lord, I was a very negative person. Anyone in my family who wanted to get close to me could not. I was always mistrustful, even with my mother whom I most loved. She considered me a "prodigal son."

Although I was born into a Buddhist family, I was not a Buddhist. After I graduated from the college of mathematics in Hanoi, I became a teacher in Haiphong and have taught there for 24 years. My students are from 13 to 50 years old. I

---

[1] "Tin Lanh" (Good News) is the official name given to all Protestant churches in Vietnam. These churches are forced to register under that name.

have also taught in secondary school and for the HO officers, the key propaganda officers in the Haiphong government. They are like the chairmen, overseeing the people in a community, and are all members of the Communist Party.

In my teaching, I wanted to be good to everyone, but my co-workers tried to find ways to step on others so that they could be promoted. Everyone was seeking approval, and their reward came by taking advantage of each other. I was cheated and deceived in many ways. I felt like they were pointing arrows at me, and I tried to find a way to fight back.

Seeking ways to please my own desire, I went to different bars to play in a band. I taught during the day and went to the bars at night. I drank a lot of alcohol and smoked a pack of cigarettes every day, but this didn't satisfy me. It just caused me more trouble.

Then I started working in a social, cultural organization. This gave me an opportunity to investigate different religions. However, I found many hypocrisies in religion. They speak about good things in the pagoda (a Buddhist temple), but out in society they don't do what they say.

In December 1989, I came to a Tin Lanh church. I met with the pastor's wife, and she told me about the gospel. Every day I would go to the library in the church to read more about the Lord. At first my purpose was only to learn about different religions, but I received the love of God from the pastor's wife as she shared the gospel with me.

At that time, the church didn't have any Bibles. Only the pastor's wife had a Bible, which she let me borrow for three days. I read as much as I could about the Lord and saw it was true. Then on February 2, 1990, I decided to receive the Lord into my heart. The Lord took away my negative feelings; I began to love others and no longer felt anger toward other people. I gave all my worries to the Lord. I then shared the gospel with my wife, and she also received Jesus in her heart. We were baptized on September 12, 1990.

Before I became a Christian, I despised my wife because she was not well educated about the world. She also rejected me and made fun of my low wages as a teacher. The Lord healed all of the offenses between us and we no longer quarreled as we used to. Now when we have disagreements, we kneel down before the Lord and ask Him to help us. I take better care of my wife, and she takes better care of me.

The Lord not only healed my heart, but He also healed my whole body. I had a stomach sickness and a bad back. Although I was nearsighted in ninth grade, I can now read without glasses, and I no longer have pains in my stomach or my back.

I also witnessed to my mother and she came to believe in the Lord. Whenever we see each other now, we cry and pray together. I praise God for restoring the love between us.

The Cost of Knowing Christ

There are only three official church buildings in Haiphong, which has a population of more than three million. In the official church, only the preacher—the one recognized by the government—can share and preach. Anyone who wishes to lead a meeting must be on the church committee, whose seven members are all appointed by the church leadership. Details of their personal life must be given to the police. Only if the police agree can a person be on the committee.

When I shared with the Christians in Haiphong about the power of the Lord, they became very zealous in sharing the gospel with others. They became involved in different projects to build up the Body of Christ. However, during a morning service in 1991, Pastor Bui Hoanh Thu announced that some of us would be thrown out of the church building. Pastor Thu, president of the official church in the North, did not care about the Christian work. Almost every Sunday, his sermons were about the laws of the government. He has worked with the police for 30 years and has caused a lot of problems for house churches by reporting to the government the names of those who attend them. He also reported that we had connections with foreigners.

All of us were called to the police office. They requested our addresses for the report and asked how we came to believe in the Lord. They commanded us not to worship the Lord at home. We are allowed to go to the official church, but we are not free to fellowship together.

This past Christmas, I met with the PA Sixteen again. We

held a church meeting in a home. More than a hundred believers and visitors came, overflowing from inside the house to outside in the yard.

Three police came and stood in the yard, then sat and listened. Although they wore civilian clothes, everyone knew they were police. I shared the message of Christmas, about the birth of Jesus. Five people came to the Lord.

I told the police, "Christmas is a day for the whole world to celebrate; it doesn't belong to any specific person or nation. We have a right to celebrate, and we do not cause problems." We did not celebrate over the time allowed by village policy. After everyone left, the police told me they would meet with me later.

The policemen took Brother Viet, the owner of the home, to another place to talk to him. "Why do you organize meetings like this, but do not report them?" they asked. Fortunately, the police didn't question anyone else, but I have been called to the police office for questioning on other occasions.

Our church has 100 members, but we cannot apply to have an official church. We meet weekly in small groups in different homes, because we do not have room to hold a large group meeting. I host the place where we meet. My wife and I use both the traditional hymn book and the new chorus books in the house church for praise and worship. Communist Party members from Haiphong have become Christians in our church.

When Christians want to establish a new church, the police reply that the government "has laws." They work with the higher church leadership in Hanoi to "give permission." If a group of believers wants to build a church, the police say, they must fill out an application and sign it. Then the government can give permission to build a church. But in reality, it is not so. Once we were given permission to have meetings where the preacher comes and teaches. The police still took us to the police station and wrote up reports, telling us that we cannot hold meetings.

One time the police fined us 1,000,000 dong, but we didn't have it. So they lowered the price to 50,000 dong. My monthly salary for teaching is 350,000 dong, which is equal to 35 U.S. dollars. The police say if we don't give them the money, they will put us in prison. Another time, the police came and fined us 50,000 dong. All the Christians donate to help pay the fine.

One woman named An went to a house meeting in Hai-Duong, a village 60 kilometers from Haiphong. When the police came, they arrested An and interrogated her at the district police station. They kept her all day and fined her 50,000 dong. A sister in Christ, who did not attend the meeting, learned of the fine and called other believers in Haiphong to ask for the money.

Walking with the Lord

Sunday mornings we meet with other believers to worship the Lord and pray. Sunday afternoons we have a meeting in my home. Monday and Tuesday afternoons we go out sharing the gospel and following up with new converts. Non-Christian friends usually invite us to come to their homes and on many occasions we share the gospel with them. If we have new believers, we teach them how to pray and worship the Lord. Tuesday nights my whole family—wife, children, brothers, and sisters—studies the Bible book-by-book in my home. Wednesday nights we go to the church to pray. Thursday nights we have a meeting where we share the gospel. Saturdays we fast and pray all day at Brother Viet's house.

I read the Bible every morning from four to five o'clock. A Bible verse God has used in my life to give me strength is Isaiah 58:11, "The Lord will guide you continually, and satisfy your soul in drought, and strengthen your bones; you shall be like a watered garden, and like a spring of water, whose waters do not fail."

Every month I go to churches in faraway places. Sometimes I borrow a motorbike or bicycle and pedal 40 kilometers. The roads are very rough with many "chicken" and "elephant" holes. A "chicken" hole is small and an "elephant" hole is big. In the rainy season, they are full of water.

I wrap my Bible in plastic and take my sermons with me. I share the gospel in different villages and rejoice in seeing new believers get baptized. We use whatever money we have to make photocopies of tracts and encourage people to read them. After they read a tract, they return it and receive a new one. A Christian friend who works in a photocopy shop copies the tracts for us carefully and quietly.

In northern Vietnam, it can get very cold. Many times when we travel to other villages in the northern areas, we must use a boat. If we cross the river when the temperature is below freezing, I get very numb; it is difficult for me to hear and my lips become numb. But when I return home where it is warmer, my body warms up and I feel much better.

How We Live
Every day my wife has to go to the market four kilometers away to sell vegetables. Our home is near the country so the people from the country sell vegetables—lettuce and different herbs —to my wife, and she sells the vegetables to others. She puts

them on the back of a bicycle in a bamboo basket; we place a piece of wood under the basket to keep it balanced on the bicycle. Then we can carry a lot of vegetables in it, tying the basket with a large rubber band. Every day we make a profit of 15,000 to 20,000 dong (about two U.S. dollars).

Our son, Do Huy Du, is 17 and in the eleventh grade. I teach every day, and my wage is just enough to pay for our son's education and his daily meal at the school. Our daughter, Do Thi Thanh Binh, is five years old. Our mother takes care of her during the day.

We have a piece of land that is 300 square meters, and a one-room brick house with a flower garden in the front yard. Our house has electricity and our water comes from a well in the yard. I pump the water by hand in a metal bucket morning and evening. We use about 20 buckets a day. My wife cooks outside in the open with coal that we buy from men who bring it to our home.

I am very grateful to the Lord for how He brings change and love into my life. I want to share with everyone how, soon after I believed in the Lord, I experienced His love and care through many people. I desire in the coming months to quit my job so that I can be involved full-time in the work of the Lord. Truly I am very content and satisfied. Whatever I do, I will do it for the Lord.

CHAPTER 2

Evangelizing Among the Villages

A Hunger for the Word

People in the villages hunger for the Lord. In 1994, Pastor Nguyen came to preach in a village, and everyone gathered in one of the pole houses. There were 70 or 80 people crowded together. Pastor Nguyen had preached only five or six minutes when the house collapsed, breaking the one-meter support poles and falling to the ground. Some people were afraid and ran out of the house; most just held onto each other and continued listening while he preached for two hours. That's how much the people hunger for the Truth. They later built the house up again.

That's why I decided to take the gospel to them. However, the beginning of my ministry was difficult. When I met my wife, I was an idol worshipper. In 1972 we escaped from the war to Lam Dong Province where we met some missionaries who shared the gospel with us. There we met the Lord.

When I started to evangelize, we didn't have a house so

Dieu E

we stayed with my wife's parents. (In S'tieng families, the mother or mother-in-law owns the house.) One morning we cooked a little stewed rice for the children and my mother. My wife's mother took away all the rice, our little pieces of gold, and even our bowl and chopsticks. They complained about me not working and leaving the home to evangelize.

We knew it would be harmful to the work of the Lord if people kept complaining, so we moved out. Now we live in a small village of 26 families, and we have our own home and work on our own piece of land. We have two daughters and one son. Our oldest child is seven years old; our youngest is one. The children often play in the dirt around the village.

I have a house that stands on poles, with a thatched roof and a floor made of bamboo. We raise chickens under the house, and can feed them by throwing rice through the floor. Our place is near a very large rubber plantation. Some of the villagers work in this plantation to earn a living.

The Lord blessed our piece of land, so that our annual crop is 100 sacks of rice, which the Lord helped multiply. We are prosperous with what we have.

Now that we have our own home and land, my mother-in-law is more friendly. People know the blessing of the Lord is upon us.

Multiplying the Word

Missionary Bet Dieu Huynh and I shared the gospel with a man from the S'tieng tribe who then shared with the tribe. We went to the Binh Duong area and found some Christians at Hoang Oanh. I shared the Word with them. They believed in the Lord but their lives did not bear any fruit. There were other believers from the city who also taught me how to study the Bible.

There were no believers in the Thanh An area, so I went there to share the gospel. Many came to know the Lord. After I left, the police came and took pictures of the Christians and showed a government film to pressure the people into not following the gospel.

The police questioned everyone in the village. They threatened them, but didn't do anything. The police tried to find the one who first brought the gospel to them. If they mentioned my name, I would be arrested. One of the new believers in his confusion and fear hanged himself.

Then the police came to my home village. The villagers told them I had gone to evangelize, since I wasn't at home. So the city police, district police, and village police went looking for me.

I was drinking iced tea in a cafe in the Thanh An area when ten policemen with pistols surrounded me. They arrived with eight crowded into a jeep and two on Honda motorbikes. The road was very dusty.

I used to work in the village office as the vice-director of the land cooperative, so one of the policemen on motorbike knew me. However, I had two names. The government knew me as Cuong, which was my name on paper, but the people in the village at home call me "E." When the police came, they asked, "Are you 'E'?"

I gave them my ID card. The man who knew me said to the other policemen, "You must be careful. This brother is Mr. Cuong; we know him in the village." So when they thought that I was not Mr. E, they returned to the village and continued to investigate.

A Visit from General Linh

During this time, a revival broke out, but the people were not yet mature or strong in the Word. Noticing an excitement among the people, the police hurried into the different areas where miracles were occurring so they could take pictures. When I went to this area to encourage the people, the police followed me.

Then the Lord moved me to another village. I continued to go from village to village to encourage the people and equip them in the Word. Since many places have opened up to the gospel and I cannot go to all of them, the people have taped my preaching and brought it to other places. We have a cassette player that does not need batteries; it has a handle that we turn by hand, generating the power it needs to run. We also duplicate many cassette tapes of sermons and share them with the tribes.

The police had confiscated one of these cassette tapes. They continued to look for me while we played "hide and seek" for six months. Finally, they came into my old village and found me.

I went out with Brother Tai, the brother of the one who hanged himself, to share the gospel. After I shared the Word with the people, I asked Brother Tai to share in the meeting. I went out to guard the back door and saw a general, the highest police rank in the district, walking through the fenced gate around the hut. It was my uncle, General Linh! But at first he didn't recognize me.

"Who's that?" he yelled.

I responded, "Me, Uncle Linh. Where are you going?"

He said, "I am going to visit your mother."

The general wanted to pass through this house where the brothers and sisters were meeting. But I redirected him, "That way is very far. Go this way," and led him outside.

He passed by the meeting place where more than a hundred people had gathered. (Many people can fit in these bamboo houses; when a family member visits, they usually stay in your home.) The Lord did a miracle at that moment. General Linh looked in and saw only one or two people, and thought they were the family of the home. The Lord blinded him to the others.

Five policemen kept looking for me. They wanted to catch me "in the act" of preaching. I continued to evangelize and hold Bible studies.

A few days later, I was planting rice when a soldier in the village brought a piece of paper, an order for me to report to the police station. I have two pieces of land, but I finished farming one piece of land. When I came in from the field, my wife's mother gave me the paper. I knew that this paper would cost me more than a few days in jail, because they had searched for me for a long time already. I went to the village police who arrested me. My family and the Christian workers stayed at home and prayed for me.

I had to report to the police station three days in a row. They claimed I had killed Brother So'Rem, who had committed suicide. But they could not prove it. I was questioned at the police station from morning until night. I was released at the end of each day, then had to report the following morning.

They brought me to the district police. They forced me to walk the four or five kilometers, not allowing me to ride in a jeep. Two policemen rode on Honda motorcycles beside me.

A colonel then interrogated me. He had two stars on each shoulder and on his collar, and he sat behind a large desk. The colonel brought out a Bible and asked, "Do you know what this is?"

I said, "Yes, I am a Christian. I know this is the Bible."

The colonel asked many questions, then said, "If you believe in this Bible, it's all right, but you are not allowed to go and evangelize. You go to evangelize and you kill people—you killed So'Rem," referring to the man who hanged himself.

That day the Vietnamese colonel handed me over to a new S'tieng policeman named Dieu Kich. He was a tribal policeman who questioned me for two days. I walked back and forth each day, a ten-kilometer round trip from my home.

On the final day, the colonel questioned me again. He looked through all my written reports and saw how each one was the same. He said angrily, "You memorize everything and then you write it down." He hit me on the head, grabbed my beard, and pushed me down on the floor. Soldiers were standing outside while the colonel beat me.

I didn't feel any hatred for this man. I still loved him, so I moved away from him and said, "In the name of Jesus." The colonel fell backwards and started shaking, then he ran out of the room.

The people outside closed the door and kept me there. I started to pray to the Lord, crying my heart out. I remembered all the places where I had gone to evangelize and gave every person to the Lord.

The colonel opened the door. He came in again but could not stay in the room, his own office. He kicked me out of his office and made me stay outside in the rain.

I said, "This July is a rainy season. It has rained very much." I asked another policeman to let me in, but I was not allowed.

The colonel went to look for other policemen, but no one wanted to work with me. They had seen the colonel running away from me. Finally the colonel said, "Now, you go and eat. I will give you some money."

I was fasting at that time, so I replied, "Why? You are not finished working with me. I will not eat."

The colonel said to me, "If you don't want to eat, you can go home."

Some days later I was back at the market and saw the colonel. I greeted him, "Mr. Buong."

He looked at me, then looked down, very ashamed. He still will not even look at me although I want to be friendly with him.

I went back home and continued to lead the people in the village. Then I started to evangelize in the Phuoc Long area, where Brother Linh was arrested. That same day, I was arrested at his sister's house.

Expanding His Borders

In 1993, I went to Bu Dop near the border of Cambodia to evangelize. This area used to belong to the French who wanted to buy land to establish rubber plantations, but it did not work out because the people there were Communists and were against any Western government. This area of Bu Dop is very large in comparison to other villages. It is very mountainous and heavily forested.

No one used to dare coming into this village, so the people are very segregated from the rest of Vietnam. Since this village is near the Cambodian border, it has both S'tieng and Khmer people. Therefore, they have intermarried and travel back and forth across the border often. They can speak S'tieng, Vietnamese, and Khmer.

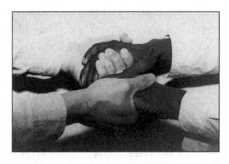

We still have not entered into the Cambodian area yet, but have shared with some people who are working in the jungles. The Lord uses these people—both S'tieng and Khmer—to enter into these isolated villages. Some live near Vietnam; some are in very remote areas in the forest on the border. Many evangelists have been arrested in this area.

If there are 20 Christian families in a village, the official church will assign one worker there and instruct him, "Whenever the house church comes here to evangelize, you have to report this to the police, so they can arrest them." If the village had no Christians, the government would not assign a worker there. They just wanted to keep whatever sheep belong to the house churches.

In these villages, the people change very slowly. They work, hunt animals, or farm on the hill. Their way of life is very slow, and they are very slow at times in receiving the Word and growing in the Lord. Some can read Vietnamese, some cannot. The city evangelistic teams give us Bibles that they receive from The Voice of the Martyrs. The teams give Bibles to those who can read Vietnamese; to others, they share the gospel and explain how to grow in Christ.

In 1995 I started to train new workers to go out and evangelize. Now when the people receive Jesus, we burn down the idols and charms of the new Christians from morning to night, and we pray for the witch doctors.

Many just don't understand the gospel. They believe that they are forsaking their homeland if they follow it. They say, "If we believe in this religion, it means we believe in some other country, a foreign religion." There was one village I visited that was very afraid. One new Christian said, "Wherever you go, I want to be just like you."

I said, "No, not like me, you must be like Jesus."

My favorite Bible verses are John 14:1–7. " 'Let not your heart be troubled; you believe in God, believe also in Me. In My Father's house are many mansions; if it were not so, I would have told you. I go to prepare a place for you. And if I go and prepare a place for you, I will come again and receive you to Myself; that where I am, there you may be also. And where I go you know, and the way you know.' Thomas said to him, 'Lord, we do not know where You are going, and how can we know the way?' Jesus said to him, 'I am the way, the truth, and the life. No one comes to the Father except through Me. If you had known Me, you would have known My Father also; and from now on you know Him and have seen Him.' "

The Communists here say that the gospel comes from the enemies. They use politics to control the people, because when the people know the Lord, there is no more fear. Christians are no longer under bondage when they become the children of God. They live under the Bible's law, not the Communists' law.

CHAPTER 3

Our Home in the Graveyard

A Godly Heritage

My father, Vu Van Yet, was imprisoned for many years for his faith in Christ. He was beaten so cruelly that both of his lungs were nearly destroyed, but he survived by the power of the Lord. For many years, he quietly carried on his lay ministry in Thuong Trang. Today he is 81 years old and cannot travel far. He is still an active Christian in an official church. His heart overflows with testimonies of how the Lord is working in the lives of the people in Thuong Trang. He wants the brothers and sisters to know how the Lord poured out His love upon the church. This is the story of his faith and the faith of the Body of Christ in North Vietnam...

My father was raised a Buddhist. He received the Lord when he was 35 years old. At that time, he worked for the French colonial government. He was arrested in 1954 and imprisoned for four years because he refused to forsake the faith.

He was also serving the Lord in an official church in Thuong

Vu Thi Muoi

17

Trang. The police arrested other believers along with my father, hoping to scare the church and stop its growth.

In the North, it was difficult to carry on the work of the Lord. From 1954 to 1975, there were no Bible schools open in North Vietnam. There were not enough pastors to serve the Lord. Some were arrested; others were banished far away. Some were forced to go into the South.

Many Christians were arrested, and many churches were closed down in the North. Many of the churches that were not closed lacked the leadership needed to survive on their own. However, the Lord watched over them, and there were people who were still faithful and did not forsake Him. Though the persecution caused problems, it also brought faith to the ones who were left behind, including my family.

My mother didn't know where the authorities had taken my father. While he was in prison, she raised my seven brothers and sisters by herself. (I am the youngest.) My mother worked in the fields. When we weren't working, we worshipped God. We read the Bible with our true hearts and prayed together.

Because our family's property was confiscated, we lived in the graveyard.
I was born there. It was very lonely for our family. The Lord kept us alive.

Because our family's property was confiscated, we lived in the graveyard. I was born there. It was an isolated place with no houses, far away from the villages. The ground was very bare with mounds of dirt. There were no grave markers, and it was surrounded by water. It was very lonely for our family.

We lived in this graveyard for seven years. The Lord kept us alive. Many people secretly brought us rice.

Our home was made of banana leaves that we cut to make a tent so the rain would not get us wet. Sometime later, Mother built a home with a thatched roof.

Twelve men had gone to prison with my father. They had worked in the French colonial government, so were accused of being counterrevolutionaries. Ten of these men died in prison. My father and another man, the only two Christians, lived. The water in prison was so terrible that it damaged my father's liver. When he was released from the prison, he was very sick. Over time, the Lord healed him.

Other people didn't want to have anything to do with us because we were Christians and the family of a former prisoner. Our relatives also did not visit us; they were afraid that visiting us would cause problems for them. When I was six years old, I recall how the Communists encouraged neighboring villagers to oppress us. They would surround us during the day and then shout accusations at us during the night. The people cursed my father. I remember hearing their voices around our grass and leaf house chanting, "Down with this man! Down with this man!"

These villagers wanted to suffocate and isolate our family. They didn't want my brothers to have an education. They wanted to squeeze us to death, to pressure us to a point of denying our faith. We were ordered not to leave the area, but my older brothers walked 25 kilometers to Haiphong where a pastor secretly gave them an education. When my brothers were in the city, they pushed very heavy carts in the streets to earn money. When they were ready to come back and visit us, they would walk only at night, avoiding the main road. They knew that if they were caught, they would be arrested. I remember seeing my brothers come back at night, entering our house in the graveyard.

But one time, one of my brothers was caught. When I was very young, I remember being awakened early one morning by many voices shouting outside. I saw one of my brothers dash out of the house and climb up the bamboo tree. The police came into the yard and made him climb down. They told him he could not go back to the city. He had to stay at our home in the graveyard under their control.

My sisters and I were not educated. My oldest sister had to work to help my mother feed us children. Because our mother had to work in the fields, she couldn't watch the two youngest boys, so she would lock them in the house for safety. During that time, we experienced how the Lord protected us all. We have had many ups and downs in life, but are thankful to the Lord for His protection and provision.

When my brother was 37 years old and studying to be a teacher, he said that our family was not under the Communists' authority, but under the authority of the Lord. The Lord gave him an opportunity later to return to Haiphong. So the police could not trace him, my brother changed his name, as our father's history was not acceptable with the government, and he moved to another district to work.

Some of my brothers escaped to Hong Kong on a small boat. They traveled for 17 days. My brothers wanted the whole family to join them, but we could not go. They now want to come back to serve the Lord here. My oldest brother is studying at a Bible school in the Hong Kong refugee camp. One brother returned to Vietnam, forsaking the possibility of greater financial opportunities, and serves the Lord here.

Hearing the Gospel
I grew up in the official church. Many pastors were, and still are, under the control of the government. They are not free to preach the Word. If they apply being a "doer of the Word,"

they will be dismissed from the church. Pastors say that Jesus is the Savior, but their sermons have to be approved by the police. Even in meetings there are always policemen present in civilian clothing. So what they share about the Word is very limited. The police keep a list of the deacons and members; church members can receive only a cloudy Christianity, because they hear about the Lord Jesus vaguely as the sermons are very limited and watered down.

In this religious atmosphere, I saw Jesus as a "god" in this world. That's why nothing changed in my life. I was involved in many activities of the church such as choir and youth group. I viewed church as my family's religion, because I hadn't met Jesus as my Savior and I didn't understand the sermons.

When I was 25 years old, I decided to follow the Lord. I would meet often with friends who were truly seeking Jesus. This caused problems in my church, as my pastor was unable to control our meetings. He called each one of us to his office and told us that we would be ex-communicated if we continued these meetings. We knew that even though the pastor ex-communicated us, God would not ex-communicate us.

My husband is a truck driver. After an accident four years ago, he was brain damaged and is not able to drive. I have to work very hard. I sew for people three or four hours every morning, so I can pay for education and food for our two children. I used to sew in a shop, but it limited my ministry in the house church and my ability to help the poor. Now I like sewing for others at home so I have more free time.

How Lovely on the Mountains
During this time, I did some work in the house church. The Lord reminded me not to forget those in other churches, so I found ways to encourage them. The places I go to evangelize are many kilometers away. Because these brothers and sisters do not have a church building, they meet in their homes. There are some house churches that have 100 members.

House church Christians are usually baptized in a lake in the mountains or in a bathtub either in one of our homes or in a hotel. When we baptize, many times the police find out and watch us. It is easy for the police to find out about our baptisms, as we come together in the village first and pray and sing songs, pouring out our hearts before the Lord. Then we go to the place where we baptize. We do not keep our prayers silent. We have been arrested many times for this.

The first time I was arrested, we were praying together on Elephant Mountain, more than 30 kilometers north of Haiphong City. We sat on the mountain slope on the grass. The weather was very hot, like fire pouring down, but big clouds came and covered the sun to shade us while we worshipped. We cried out before the Lord, praying for the situation in Vietnam, and gave our hearts to serve God. We prayed for five hours. The people around the mountain heard us singing.

In the evening, we returned to the city. A policeman came to my house with an arrest warrant, ordering me to report the next day to the Cabinet, a national security organization. This was the first time I ever went to the police, as my family and I never broke the law. I was quite worried. That night I prayed and could not sleep. I kneeled down and cried to the Lord saying, "In your Word You say that You are greater than any god in this world." And then I opened the Bible and the Lord spoke to me in Isaiah 43. The Lord said that when we walk through the waters and through the fire, we will not be overcome. So after I prayed, I found peace and slept well.

The next morning, I went to the police office with joy. It was a one-and-a-half-kilometer ride on my bike. I rode up to the center of national security in Haiphong, a large brick building painted yellow. I parked my bicycle at the gate and showed the arrest papers. Walking through the main gate, I went into the building looking for the room to which I was ordered to report.

Two policemen greeted me very coldly. I sat on one side of a long table and they sat on the other side. I prayed that the

Lord would give me the boldness and would help me to look straight into the face of these people. I didn't hate them because of the work they had to do. The Lord had given me a love for them, and I knew this time would be an opportunity for me to preach the gospel. They questioned me about many things. When I started sharing about the Word of God, four other police-

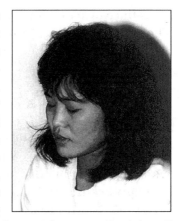

men came in. They had been in the nearby room listening. I shared the gospel in tears.

They questioned me for two hours, "Why do you believe in God?" I told them about Jesus, how the Lord is good and how He has saved my life. I focused on God's love toward man. I could tell that they were very interested in what I had to say.

They asked me why I went to the mountainside instead of a church building. I replied, "God is everywhere, so we can worship God anywhere we want. Because the mountainside is very beautiful, very quiet, we want to save the most beautiful place for worshipping God."

In the beginning they were very furious, but later they were persuaded by the love of God. I forgot that they were policemen. I also forgot about the dangers I might face. I desired that the Lord would bring them to His love, just as I have been brought to His love.

At the end of the talk, one policeman asked me, "If now we want to believe in God, is it possible?" I said, "Yes, anytime."

I have shared the gospel with 15 policemen and with many other people I meet on the street. I have gone to the police many times and always see new ones in different offices and police stations. The police never have me talk with the same policemen each time, because they know I will convince them to become a Christian.

In the North they force us to go to official church meetings. They want us to meet in the church building, not in homes. The government gives orders to the official churches that if we gather more than five people in a home at one time, they can arrest us.

In Haiphong they do not fine Christians, they arrest us. There is a saying that "we can put a hat on a person," which means to falsely accuse the person of a social or political crime (not a religious crime). The government gives the religious crime a "different hat." This happens many times.

This week no one is in jail, but many are threatened and pressured. Newly ordained pastors in the North and pastors with a soft heart to preach the gospel are moved to a remote area. This even happens to the official church pastors. The government also tries to control pastors by giving them money. They try to discourage the work any way they can.

Bibles are few. Only the people in church leadership have a Bible. Usually brothers and sisters in the North receive Bibles from Christians in the South. We also send money to Christians in the South to buy Bibles for us when they are available through the official church. Sometimes we receive Bibles free from other countries. Pastor Thu tried to sell one of these Bibles for 20,000 dong (a day's wages), but they usually are not sold to house church members. In Hanoi, house churches meet in different groups. These Christian workers know each other, so we can share Bibles with them.

The officials claim that all religions are equal, but actually they discriminate to cause problems for the students. I am 36 years old and have two sons: a 15-year-old who serves the Lord in a youth group, and an 11-year-old. If they meet at the official church, they will have no problems in school. But if they meet with the house church, there will be a problem. If anyone follows a religion, it will affect their place in society by determining their work.

I ride as much as 40 kilometers on my bicycle to share the gospel with people in different villages. My brother directs an orphanage, and we share the gospel in a school. The Bible verse that I always remember is 1 John 4:8, "God is love." We wish to win as many people as possible to the Lord through His love. My ministry requires a lot of my time, but it is worth it.

I am very grateful to have an opportunity to meet with the servants of God from other countries and to know that the Lord is opening doors for the gospel in Vietnam, especially in North Vietnam. On behalf of my brothers and sisters in Christ in North Vietnam, we appreciate "unofficial" missionaries who come to Vietnam and also the evangelistic teams here. I know that this is God's hand. I pray that the Holy Spirit will help all to understand the work the Lord is doing here. I don't see the boundary of races or nationalities. I see that everyone has one Father, and I want to say to the other brothers and sisters from far away that the Holy Spirit is visiting Vietnam.

CHAPTER 4

Motorbike Messengers

And You Shall Bear Fruit...

Before 1975 one tribe had only two Christians. Many tribal villagers were very amazed, because usually a tribal person like me, who lives near the national road, will not go into a remote area deep in the jungle for any reason. After Brother E received a vision, we went together to this particular tribe. In less than four months, the church there grew to 150.

The only Bible that the people had was a pocket New Testament. Usually a few main workers have the Old and New Testaments. Only one family per village typically has a Bible.

Since they have no kerosene for lighting, they burn pinewood. They place the pinewood sticks in a big metal dish and hang it from the ceiling. Usually, they hang two in a room. Even with this light, it is difficult to read.

The ceilings in the houses of the tribal brothers are usually low. We have to stoop as we go through the door, and we do not have enough light because these firebowls cannot be placed high. The long houses have rough and bumpy dirt floors. Many times snakes and other creatures like centipedes

K'Be

come into the houses, but we are not bitten. The walls and roof are made of thatch, and the roof is held up with poles. The houses have a kitchen area at one end and the water is outside.

Everyone packs into a house about nine meters wide by nine meters long. Usually 70 or 80 people are crowded together. The owner of this house added on to it with more grass and bamboo so more people can meet together. It's cold in there. Everyone wraps in a blanket and sits side by side. The Christians gather at night to sing, and they memorize songs by heart. The Lord gives them strength to serve Him well.

The people sit far away from the light so the dropping ashes will not burn them. Usually the heavy smoke spreads all over the room, blackening the walls and roof. Many times after a meeting, the people who come from far away stay overnight. In the morning they leave for their homes farther in the jungle. Only their eyes are visible because their faces are black with ash and smoke. Those who live nearby return to their homes at night and sometimes take others with them to rest.

On one occasion, some of the villagers gave a false report about me to the government. They told them that I was involved in anti-government, secular work, destroying ancestor worship and idols that the people had followed for years.

In June 1994, the police ordered me to their office. The Word says that whoever finds his life will lose it, and he who loses his life for His sake will find it (Matthew 10:39). I praised the Lord, because in the Scripture it is written that the godly man will have to be persecuted.

I was called to the police station three more times because weak Christians under persecution told them about me. One brother said, "Brother K'Be gave it to me." Four house churches in different villages reported that I was the one who gave them Bibles.

As I entered the police station, the police said, "Today we will give you time to think it over. Are you willing to speak the truth today? We have all these papers as proof against you."They handed me a piece of paper that a brother had placed inside his Bible. The paper had my name on it. They told me to open my eyes wide to see if it was my name.

When I looked at it, I saw that the piece of paper was mine, but the wrong tribe was written. I replied honestly, "That is not my tribe." So the Lord opened a way for my release.

Afterward, the police came to persecute two village churches that I had established in this area. These believers were the first spiritual harvest that the Lord gave me. I was very happy and often visited to encourage the brothers. Then the persecution came abundantly, shaking the church.

Knowing God's Voice

My work has been successful because of the wholehearted support from my wife, Kiop. She prays for me as I minister, and she takes care of the children. We have two kids still in school. Our youngest daughter is nearly five years old and very cute. Our son is nine. Many times my wife joins me on a trip, sometimes for days, and we leave the children with my wife's sister who takes good care of them.

Kiop handles children's evangelism. We are happy serving the Lord. With this ministry, there is much persecution and many joys. Many times our income is not as good as the others who focus their time working on plantations, but the Lord gives us enough for daily life.

Whenever I go to evangelize, my wife and I usually pray together and see how the Lord leads us together. One Sunday morning, I planned to go to the Phu Hiep church to share the Word. I woke up early and told my wife, "We must get up early and go by bicycle to the Phu Hiep church and have communion there."

My wife, as the Lord moved in her heart, said, "This morning, I don't feel we should go to Phu Hiep church." I agreed, and we decided to go the following week.

Bible Raid

Later that day, a brother from that church ran to our home
and said, "Oh, Brother K'Be, what should we do now? This
morning, a special team of police poured into our home where
we were meeting. The brothers hadn't yet handed out the
Bibles; they were still hanging in the bags on the wall. The
police just rushed in and took everything. They were very
cruel."

These tribal people have very simple houses. They keep
their Bible in a bag that hangs on the wall. The police looked
in the bags and took six Bibles, but there were other Bibles
that the brothers quickly hid.

Earlier in the day, the police caught three new converts in
Don Duong who had been Christians for only three months,
including Brother Nhien. The police had tried to find me
when they caught these Christians and ordered them to report
to the police station on Tuesday. They went to the church at
Phu Hiep that Sunday and asked, "Where is Mr. K'Be?" I was
grateful that my wife urged me not to go to Phu Hiep that day.

I was called to the police station the next morning. Before
I went, I met Brother Nhien who told me, "It was good that you
didn't come on Sunday morning. They looked for you, and
they called me to go to the police tomorrow."

We talked together, deciding what to say. I encouraged
him, "Don't be afraid. The Lord will be with you and help you.
Be careful, because they will say that Mr. K'Be told them about
you already. But this will be a lie to trick you."

Later the police sent an order for all the male Christians in
the Phu Hiep church to go to the police office, where they
were arrested. For the first week, they were isolated in a dark
cell without food or drink. The following week, Brother
K'Nhin was placed in cell number three, which is a special
room where all the prisoners use the toilet. The Christians
could not eat much rice because of the smell. Brother K'Nhin
had to stay in that cell for a week. After his release from prison,
he was seriously ill for three or four months. I was never in that

cell, but the police threatened me, "If you do not give an accurate report, then tonight we will let you see what it is like in room number three."

The police told these Christians that they didn't report clearly because they covered for me. These faithful believers didn't want to say that I was the one who comes to help their church, so they remained silent.

The month of June is harvest time so it is very difficult. There was no more food in the homes from the previous harvest and the villagers had just started to harvest the new crop. The Christian families were also lacking food, but they still brought food into the prison for the men. I encouraged the church to leave gifts of food for those in prison.

The police did not allow the church members to communicate with the brothers in prison, because they were afraid that they would exchange counsel and opinions. So the wives would just leave a woven basket with rice for their husbands. Every two days, they would also try to bring vegetables. However, the police took the vegetables and would slide under the door only rice and salt.

After this persecution, the Christians' faith was a bit shaken, so they sent word that I could no longer come to their village or they would be persecuted more. So I sent word to them that the Lord says in Matthew 11:6, "Blessed is he who keeps from stumbling over Me," and many more words to encourage them. A while later they invited me to come back again. I came and encouraged the church so now the church is as strong as before.

After the police arrested the three brothers from Don Duong and didn't get any information from them, they fined them 750,000 dong (two or three months' wages) and released them. The Christians didn't have the money, so they ran to me and asked, "Where can we borrow some money? Perhaps after we are released from the prison interviews, we can work in the forest to cut down logs or do something to pay someone back."

Usually in a small village the tribal people don't have money and have to borrow from the Vietnamese. If the Christians cannot pay the fine, then the police will sentence them to two months in prison. Many times they borrow from the nonbelievers, and have to pay a high interest rate. If they borrow 100,000 dong, for example, then in six months they must repay 170,000. Six months is a short time to pay off the loan. Christian families pay what they can. It depends on the mood of each nonbeliever. If they have much, they give much.

Some Christians pay them back by raising cocoons for silk. Some people saw logs; others give one day's wages in a plantation to help raise money for the brothers.

I told these Christians that my main work was to help serve the Lord, so I didn't have much money. We prayed together, and then the Lord provided us with the exact amount of money from Christian friends in the city—750,000 dong. The Christians were released. I praised the Lord that no one had to go to prison because they were unable to pay the fine.

These brothers learned in prison that when they rely on man, man cannot help, so they rely on God. The Lord can open different ways to help them. The Lord gives them strength to serve Him well.

Baptism of Mud

Last April during the night, a brother led us on motorbike to a village to visit the Long Quac church. My wife and I followed him on a second motorbike; she rode on the back. We brought along Bibles and tracts.

We had to ride up and down hills on roads with big holes and sneak into the village. I have a light on my motorbike, but many times I ride at night without my light for safety. I use a flashlight in case I don't remember the road well. I asked my wife to turn on the flashlight for just one minute and then turn it off and keep going.

We could only see stars and the motorbike light or flashlight sneaking through the village, not knowing where to go. But since this brother knew the way, he led us.

In the rainy season, it is very easy to fall. Sometimes the roads are so wet and muddy that we cannot push our motorbikes through them. Many times we fall in the water. One night, we were on a muddy road moving quite fast through the puddles of water. We had a light, but the road was too slippery. We crossed some sticky mud and fell over on the side. Another sister in Christ also fell. We told her to sit still while we slowly pushed the motorbike back up for her. We were very dirty with red mud all over us.

Our trip takes a long time. We have to stop and use a stick to push away all the mud that gets stuck on the fenders and wheels. Then we push the motorbike and continue on, but mud gets stuck all over the wheels again.

We usually arrive at the village hours later. We have to visit them at night, because during the day they work 20 kilometers away. The people burn a fire inside the house on the dirt floor and put out some hot water for tea. Everyone sits and waits for us. We visit and sometimes pray for the sick, share Scripture, and stay there a few hours. Then we go home before the police notice. We turn off the motorbike light and sneak out quickly.

One night we were going across the region from Quang Khe, crossing over the district of Lam Dong Province. There is a river in this area. We were walking on a trail in the jungle forest where there were tigers and monkeys. When we walk in the jungle, we walk single file, with one person in front of the other. Usually the tribal people have cut the grass to show the way. That night, one brother walked in front of me and another brother in back, carrying a machete (a long knife).

We heard sounds like something stepping on sticks and bamboo trees. So I said, "Is that a tiger?" and the brother in front responded, "No, not so." But I turned around and spotted a tiger on the right. I saw its yellow and black stripes. We said, "Oh, God will protect us. Just walk." So we just walked.

My favorite verse, John 15:16, is how the Lord called me: "You did not choose Me, but I chose you and appointed you that you should go and bear fruit." I ask that the brothers and sisters in other countries remember to pray especially for my tribe, the K'ho tribe, and for Vietnam in general, so that the gospel will be freely preached and His kingdom will expand. We also remember to pray for you, brothers and sisters.

CHAPTER 5

House Churches Spreading

A Change of Heart, Mind, and Hands

When I was a policeman, I met a preacher whom we called in for questioning about his religious activities. As a policeman, we watched the Que Son and Da Nang areas closely where Communism is much stronger than around Ho Chi Minh City[2] (Saigon). My area, Que Son, is known to be one of the most difficult areas in Da Nang Province.

I noticed that there were men who followed the Christian religion, but they didn't act like it. They were committing many crimes. We called in the pastor because these Christians were in his church; we wanted to reprimand him. The officials had me handle this case.

I had worked with social crimes such as violence, theft, and homicide. In some cases, we would accuse people so we could just mark the crime off a chart and finish that case. Many Christians wouldn't talk much because they were afraid of me. But this pastor was not afraid.

I was curious. When I asked him about religious matters, he gave me a gospel tract. He told me stories and many other things in the Bible, so many that I couldn't remember them all. I wanted to hear more.

---

[2] After the Communist takeover in 1975, the city of Saigon was renamed Ho Chi Minh City. Many Vietnamese living in the South use either name when referring to the city.

We talked for three hours. He was very polite and humble. I observed his attitude, the way this preacher slowly shared the gospel with me while I sat quietly beside my desk. He acted very upright. Whether he had committed a crime or not, he seemed to be a righteous man. I had a joyful time visiting with him.

Not long after that meeting, I started going to church. The other policemen who worked with me did not know about this. I would ride my bicycle to the church during the day. I wasn't afraid. I wanted to go so much that I didn't care if I got caught.

Not knowing what a church was, I sat in the pastor's home enjoying the beautiful songs they would sing. I didn't know these songs or understand them, but I listened to them intently.

Linh holding a Bible

The pastor would invite me to eat in his home. He was not afraid of me, but I could tell that the others were. Perhaps they were afraid because I was a policeman, but I don't know their hearts.

I went to church regularly, but I did not know God yet. After a year, the pastor was transferred to another location, so I became greatly discouraged and stayed home.

However, after five months of not having a Bible, I hungered for the Word and prayed. Finally I met some workers of an evangelistic team who had been trained in the Word. I had invited the Lord into my heart, but did not know for sure until these Christian workers shared with me. Now I did not worry about my job. Following the Lord is forever; my police job was only temporal. Whatever the Lord gives me, I will be happy with that.

My favorite verse is, "All Scripture is given by inspiration of God, and is profitable for doctrine, for reproof, for correction, for instruction in righteousness" (2 Timothy 3:16). The Lord gave me an opportunity to meet with these Christian brothers to pray and study the Word for a year. I was seeing the Lord work in my life.

The Lord also healed me. My hand was swollen very badly, and we had no money for treatment. So I prayed and said, "I have no money. So, Lord, as you healed many Israelites in the Old Testament, would You heal me also?" The Lord healed my hand immediately.

On the Other Side of the Table

I was originally in the army and then was transferred to the police. After working in the police office for 12 years, I was notified that the police wanted to dismiss me. They didn't give me a reason. Some police said, "Now that you have God, you must sit aside." They put me in an office where I was isolated from my co-workers. They didn't give me any more work to do. I became very bored, so I quit.

After I left my profession, I started to farm a small piece of land that I had. I planted some white potatoes and rice. We live in a mud house with a thatched roof. The kitchen is next to the house. We cook with dry branches and every day carry water 500 meters from other people's wells, because we don't have a well yet. We used to have kerosene, but 12 days ago electricity was put in my home.

Our house is near a mountain, so during the night I hear many animals—tigers, deer, ravens, and many others that live in the jungle. I also hear crickets. We keep our window open so the moon can shine in. The wind blows through our one-room house.

The house is very empty. We have beds made with bamboo—one bed for the children and one for my wife and me. We have a woven mat on our bed. We must use good bamboo to last a long time, or the beds will just collapse.

Recently we had a flood, so all of the rice crop my wife and I planted has been destroyed. The flood did not harm the houses in the area, only the lower field.

Our whole family attends church. I have two daughters, one in ninth grade and one in first grade. Some of my friends said that since I would no longer join them in drinking, they would not have anything to do with me. But I have become even better friends with the people I have won to the Lord.

We use our home as a meeting place for 30 people. We don't have chairs, so we sit on the floor. House churches are not allowed to have literature, but the official church can. If the police find that a house church prints material—Bibles, hymns, songs, or anything—they take it away. We have 11 Bible lessons; we begin with our foundation in Christ, and then study repentance and faith.

The police have called me to the station twice already. The first time was when we were having a Bible study. We had 30 people in my house the evening the police came. They fined each person 2,000 dong; our people are very poor. All of us were called up to the police office. We all had to walk 30 kilometers while the four policemen followed us in a jeep. They all had guns. If a Christian was quick, he could run off the road and return home, but the ones who were slow were put in the line to walk to the police office.

There were old men and women, young men and women. Since it was summer, it was very dusty. Along the road people watched us as we went by, especially children and other Christians belonging to our group. I walked in the front.

The office of the district police is a brick building with beautiful yellow tile. All 30 of us went into a big room. The police said I was responsible, so they released all the people except for me.

Now I was sitting on the other side of the table, being questioned by the authorities but sharing the gospel with them whenever I had a chance. After questioning me for three days, they wrote up a report and released me. Some of the police were sympathetic. Many police today don't know the Bible; they just think we have a foreign religion that will influence the people. They don't know why it is spreading so quickly. They know that many Christians are good, so that's why some police are not truly angry. One time they told me to do whatever I wanted, but not to let the official church know. If the offi-

Since 1975, thousands of Christians meet secretly in homes and in the jungle, such as this group.

cial church finds out and reports to the police, these same police will then arrest us.

I kept having meetings in my home, as I have the only house church in the area.

I am thankful to the Lord. When I first came to know Him, everybody had closed their door against me. They mocked me and did all kinds of things. But now, the Lord makes many want to come visit me. They give me help to reach different villages. Even the nonbelievers lend me money so I can buy a ticket for the bus.

Sometimes I go by bicycle or by motorbike 30 to 40 kilometers away. The Lord has raised up many small groups in the villages I visit. If a brother asks me to come, I go and take Bibles with me for his house church and sleep on a floor mat for a few days. The work is spreading much among the Vietnamese, and I praise God for making me a part of the work.

CHAPTER 6

Echoes of Praise in the Jungle

The End of the Line

Tong Le Chan Prison is terrible. It is the end of the line. Many there are robbers, murderers, or guilty of social crimes. Five pastors, including me, and one social criminal were put on a Russian microbus to that prison.

The night before we left, I had a dream about a storm with a big eagle flying, but I did not understand it. When the bus reached the prison, the guard transferred us to the local officer. When we stepped out of the bus, I saw many prisoners.

They had on short pants and bare backs. On their backs all had the tattoo of an eagle. The dream that the Lord gave me was fulfilled. He gave me peace, a promise to protect me and all the pastors in this terrible situation.

The Lord has protected me in my work. The area where I and others preach the gospel is in Lam Dong, Bao Loc. It's about 200 kilometers from Ho Chi Minh City. Many people have received Jesus among the K'ho. There are 500 new believers now.

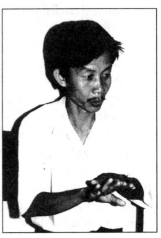

Hoang Van Phung

During the last six months of 1990, the Lord sent Christians to come and train us in the Word. During that time, the police arrested three preachers who had taught us for five days. The three preachers arrested were Brother Hoa, Brother Hoang, and Brother No. They were imprisoned for two months and each fined 100,000 dong. My co-worker and neighbor, Brother Vu Minh Xuan, and I were later called to the police station several times over many months.

Then in early January 1991 when I returned from sharing the gospel, the police surrounded my house and Brother Xuan's house next door. There were five or six police in the jeep. One ran straight into my house and said, "Stand up!" He had a piece of paper with the words "Urgent Arrest."

I had only a few minutes to say goodbye to my wife and children, and then they handcuffed me and took me to the jeep. Brother Xuan was also arrested. They took us to the prison in the district province where they kept us for 22 days.

They questioned me many times. They told me that Christianity is an American religion and that the Tin Lanh church gospel is from the CIA.

I answered them, "No, we only witness for Jesus Christ. We don't do politics."

They isolated me in a room with no light. Brother Xuan was in another cell. Days later, they also arrested a young tribal preacher, K'Philip; he was in the room next door. A long-term prisoner who brought the food told me.

Inside the prison I was very hungry for the Word of God. My wife tore out several pages of our Bible, wrapped bread around them, and gave the "package" to me. This got by the police. I hid the Word of God in my little tattered old bag, which was so bad that the police didn't look inside. I tried to find a way to contact Brother K'Philip to share some pages with him.

Later on, they transferred me to a bigger cell. Brother K'Philip was next door, so I gave him my Bible pages through the bars of the door. We would exchange a few pages with each other as we finished reading them.

Brother K'Philip, Brother Xuan, and I were put in a line together with the social criminals to be videotaped. We were considered political prisoners. The chief of police, a general in this area, told us, "I will keep you in prison for two years." Our files went to the Central Bureau, and the Domestic Affairs Bureau continued to review them.

One day they said, "Prepare your clothes and go to the jeep." While we gathered together for the trip to another prison, Brother K'Philip was worried because we kept the Bible pages inside our pockets.

I answered, "Don't worry, the Lord will protect us."

So they put us in the prison jeep, chained our hands and feet together, and videotaped us while they transferred us to Da Lat Prison 120 kilometers away. We prayed continually on the way there; we didn't know where they were taking us. Many people on buses looked down on us, thinking that we were robbers.

They stopped at a prison where criminals are held temporarily. When we reached the cell, we were with the "chief of the room." We call them the "eagles." They are older prisoners who checks on things, search bags and everything. The Lord helped us. When the "eagle" looked at the pages of the Bible, he thought that they were rotten. He crumpled them up and threw them on the floor.

An officer from the Central Bureau in Hanoi came to Da Lat to interrogate us, so we had to be brought to Da Lat City. We stayed in Da Lat, but were under the direct supervision of Hanoi Domestic Affairs. All of the officers were from North Vietnam. They were taller than me, with a lighter skin color, and speak with a different accent. They sat in green uniforms opposite me, and had many documents on my case.

When we first reached this prison, Brother K'Philip was placed in a tiny concrete cell with chains on both of his feet.

If you stand up, you can reach the ceiling. If you lie down, your head and feet touch opposite walls.

Inside K'Philip's room, he did not know if it was day or night. Each person receives ten liters of water daily for washing and everything else. K'Philip was held in his isolation cell for six months with no bath, except for the little drinking water he put on a napkin to wash himself.

Brother Xuan was put in a larger room with ten social criminals. According to "prison law," a new prisoner will be beaten and have all of his things stolen. But when Brother Xuan came in, the Lord covered him so that he wasn't beaten. The chief prisoner told Xuan to stand up, looked through all of his clothes and asked, "What crime did you commit?"

He answered, "I am a preacher of Jesus."

The prisoner laughed at him. They removed his chains and showed him the place where he must sleep. It was at the end

of the room near the toilet, very dirty.

He sat next to a young boy who had committed social crimes and was covered in lice from his head to his feet. You cannot imagine how Xuan felt! He was told to sleep near this boy where he would be attacked by the lice.

In my room I started to share the gospel. Many received Jesus and were joyful.

The police continued to call me for questioning. They charged me with spreading superstition. A policeman wrote on my chart "superstitious," and tried to force me to sign.

But I told the policeman, "I am a preacher. I share about Jesus and don't talk about superstition, so I won't sign this paper."

The policeman shoved the table and threatened to put me in an isolation cell, but I still would not sign.

The guards sent me to a small isolation cell with another prisoner who was sentenced for life for pushing a man onto a stone and killing him. Earlier Brother K'Philip had shared the gospel with this man, so I continued to follow up with him. This prisoner began to pray wholeheartedly to the Lord.

In this place it's very cold. I slept on a piece of wood near the toilet bucket. I remembered the Psalm that my wife had given me on a torn page from the Bible, Psalm 107:6, "Then they cried out to the Lord in their trouble, and He delivered them out of their distresses." In this cell, I raised my hands to the Lord, prayed and thanked Him because I believed that He would deliver me out of this place to the interrogation room.

Soon the police called me again and said, "Are you willing to sign?"

I said, "No," and they put me back in the isolation cell.

I knew the Lord heard me pray that night. He used a captain of the PC 15 to deliver me. The policeman was in charge of the temporary imprisonment of different persons in the area. When the policeman under him wanted me to remain in the isolation cell, the captain ordered, "Send him back to the bigger cell with the other social criminals."

The policeman who worked with him came to this captain and argued, "This prisoner is very stubborn. You must put him in isolation."

But the captain said, "I will be responsible for his health, so take him back to the bigger cell."

Inside the prison, it is very difficult to share the gospel because the police are always watching; they also have informers. But the Lord led me to the ones I could trust. Because this was a temporary prison, many were transferred. During the eight months that I was there, I shared the gospel with 20 prisoners. So when I came back from isolation, there were four or five Christians there. These believers happily took my hand

and hugged me. When the "eagle" checked me, this time he threw my Bible pages away, but I had memorized them.

In the Eagle's Nest
I was sent to Tong Le Chan labor camp with the other preachers, including Hao Anh, Brother K'Philip, and Brother Xuan. That's when I had the dream about a storm with a big eagle flying. The Russian bus we rode in was army green and didn't have a name to identify it. We were chained to each other, and on the back of our clothes we had to write "C.T.," which means a person being sent for "re-education."

The trip to Tong Le Chan Prison was nine hours long. We drove from early morning until about four or five o'clock in the afternoon. There were three young policemen to guard us. One knew that we were all pastors, so on the way he said, "If you want to buy bread or anything on the road to eat, I will buy it for you." They let us down to go to the toilet and, because we were pastors, they also took off our chains. But the social criminal remained bound.

We were very happy, knowing that the Lord had opened a door for us to be together. We had our own "revival" and were filled with joy as we worshipped the Lord. From a bus nearby, the people looked at us, shocked and amazed to see such joy in prisoners. The guards were sitting in the back, the front, and the middle looking at us very curiously. One policeman asked, "Why are these prisoners acting like this?"

When the bus reached the area, the guard transferred us to the local officer. Seeing the tattoos, I remembered the vision I had of the storm and the eagle. The police shaved our heads and allowed us pastors to stay together.

All of us pastors labored like the other prisoners, clearing the jungle with big machetes, sawing wood, and plowing the land. Every day the prisoners had to work hard. But the last prison director took bribes; both he and the eagles took the food so that there was not enough food for us. In the prison, we were very hungry and skinny. When there was food, we would receive only two bowls of thin soup made with rice. So in heavy labor, some prisoners could not survive, and many on the labor line fainted.

That's why the prisoners would stab one another, fighting for food. When they go out to work during the day, they find wire and metal pieces from mines that had exploded in the area during the war. They hide these to make knives. Every week somebody is wounded and taken to the prison hospital.

The prisoners who had been there for a long time told us, "You guys have come here when the prison is in a peaceful state. Before you came, there was fighting and much revenge among the prisoners. Sometimes they would throw a burning plastic bag in the face of a prisoner, which would burn his face terribly." We praised the Lord because the new director, Chu Xuan Dinh, had changed the situation for the better.

The new director allowed the families of the prisoners to send food to them. The prison officials gave us 500 grams of rice per day. We would share our food with the other prisoners who received none from home.

We heard that Pastor Hung and seven other tribal preachers were arrested. Hung and the other tribal men didn't have enough food to eat, but they set a good example by doing the forced labor even though they were weak from hunger. They picked leaves off of a bush and cooked them with some vegetables, but it was not enough.

The eagles inside the camp tried to rob our things. One time an eagle noticed Preacher K'Philip's good pants and told his disciple, "Go and tell him I want to borrow his good pants."

We told him that we don't have many pants, we just have enough to wear.

They said, "Lend him yours, and he will give you his old pants." Then in a show of power, the eagle made his own disciple kneel down, took out his belt, and beat him cruelly in front of the Christians.

In one area there were four long rooms with about 200 to 300 prisoners in each one. After doing heavy labor all day, we would come back to our cell block and be under the control of the eagles. Instead of letting us rest, sleep, and pray, the eagles would create many activities to punish us. Every morning at five o'clock after the prisoners washed and groomed themselves, the eagles made everyone sit still in a line before going to work. Under the eagles' control, we suffered with heavy labor in the cell as well as outside in the fields.

When I first came to Tong Le Chan, I was assigned to a team, shoveling the land. There were 17 to 20 people in one team. Two police watched us. When I worked for a few days, the chief policeman called me and said, "Tomorrow you will go and boil water for me."

I returned to my work but didn't know what he meant. Another prisoner said, "You will be very happy to boil water because you will not do heavy labor like us. But, on the other hand, you have to buy two bags of noodles to cook for them everyday and buy cigarettes for them to use everyday. Even though you will not have to do anything, you have to use your own money to pay for all of this, including buying the tea and making the tea for them to drink."

I dreamed that night that I was pouring a sack of tea into a big container of water. In the morning I prayed to the Lord, but I didn't have peace. The Lord showed me what I was to do about this. A social criminal would be very happy to take care of this work since this was one way of bribing. But as for me, a preacher, I wouldn't do that. I went straight to the policeman and said, "I cannot do it."

He said, "Then you can go and shovel."

I told him, "I believe that the Lord will strengthen me."

The prisoners and the police were shocked, thinking that I was crazy for refusing something good like this. So they offered, "Why don't you choose a better labor place?"

The place where we worked was a fast 45-minute walk from the camp. They assigned me and some of the other prisoners to work in a dam full of shallow water. We had to clear out the weeds and grass, then prepare the area for growing rice.

One time we were all pun-
ished for a week. We had to
shovel from morning until
evening, and each prisoner
had to shovel 200 square meters of ground a day. During
the monsoon season, it rained
the whole day and we had only
short pants to wear. In this de-
serted area, there were a lot of
snakes, and centipedes and
jungle bees that stung us. At
the same time, we had to fight
with the thorns under our
feet.

The water was full of
leaches. We called them buffalo leaches, because they were as
big as a finger. We had to watch each other's skin and shovel
at the same time so that whoever saw a leach would pull it off
the other man and throw it far away.

If we could not finish the work assigned to us, the guards
put us in a prison within the prison. It's a very small place
where we could have only one glass of water and one bowl of
rice a day. There were no mosquito nets. Pastor Nguyen was
put in there for two weeks.

Exhausted, I prayed, "Lord, save me!" while I shoveled. I
meditated upon the Word because it comforted me.

Echoes of Praise

Many S'tieng tribal people lived and worked around the camp.
Their children didn't have any education. Often as they cared
for their buffalo, they walked through the areas where we
prisoners worked. Usually these children had no food. Before
we came to Tong Le Chan Prison, the people there had never
heard of Jesus. We were certain that the Lord would open the
door for us to preach the gospel to them.

When the brothers and sisters came to visit us in the prison, they started to share about their contact with the S'tieng tribe there. The S'tieng worked on the edge of the woods. Our team of Christians began to secretly share the gospel with them. Many became Christians. They have a strong faith in the Lord even though they are very poor, lacking food and clothes. Jesus changed their lives completely, and they are so joyful in the life of Jesus. Now thousands of the S'tieng people have become Christians.

We were always watched while we worked in the jungle. We could not share the gospel openly, so we had a code word when we saw the tribal people. We would say, "Hallelujah!" If one was a Christian, we would know right away because he would reply, "Hallelujah!"

A pastor from the city had privately taught them how to sing worship songs. One time while we were working and meditating on the Lord, we heard gospel songs floating out through the trees. Children were singing, making an echo all over the jungle. The Lord comforted my heart through the voices of these children.

Although the police guarded us carefully inside the prison at Tong Le Chan, we shared the gospel and many other prisoners believed in Jesus. We also shared the gospel while we were holding our shovels, standing in line to go to work. We would raise our hand and worship God while laboring in the field. We couldn't sing loud because a guard was still there, so we sang very quietly. When we ate lunch together in the field, whoever memorized a verse would tell another, thus sharing the Word of God.

The police changed things all the time. Sometimes we pastors were together in the room having our lunch, and sometimes we were scattered in different sections of the camp. We memorized many verses and shared them with each other, such as Philippians 4:13, "I can do all things through Christ who strengthens me"; Psalm 107:6, "They cried out to the Lord in their trouble, and He delivered them out of their distresses"; Psalm 23; and many others. We were very happy when we listened to the Word, because it revived us.

Some of the police called me a pig and humiliated me in different ways. But the Lord also brought some good people into the police circle who treated me very well. For example, I met a police colonel who was imprisoned for 20 years because he had helped someone escape from the country. When he met with me, he still had 15 more years to serve. He put his hand on my shoulder and told me, "You, preacher, when you go home, remember to pray for me because I have believed in Jesus in prison."

He told me that while he was still a colonel, he had arrested many preachers and pastors. He was an atheist. But the first three months he was in prison, he could not sleep.

One pastor nearby told him, "If you believe in Jesus, you will see a miracle."

That night, he kneeled down, alone, praying, "Jesus, I don't know who You are, but if it's true that Jesus is God who created this world and who created me, You give me a sign. It's been four months and I still cannot sleep. So if You are real, then give me a good sleep tonight." That night, he slept well for the first time in four months.

While in prison, we listened to Pastor Nguyen as he taught us to try different ways to share the gospel and to take care of new converts. Pastor Nguyen also had to labor very heavily in that camp. Although he suffered with rheumatism and swollen legs, he still had to walk 45 minutes each way to work in the field. Many times the pain was so great he could not hold back his tears. He walked with a stick, and somebody had to help him go to the field.

Pastor Ha Hak in the Barrel

Another Christian in prison, Lo Ban Hen, told us the story of a tribal pastor named Ha Hak. (After Lo Ban Hen was released, he was transferred to North Vietnam.) Pastor Ha Hak was put in prison many times, once for seven months. The latest news is that he has witnessed to 700 members of his tribe, and they all became Christians. Serving the Lord in the highlands is very difficult. The police always accuse pastors of "doing politics." They don't understand that this pastor is only preaching the gospel.

Once while interrogating Pastor Ha Hak, a policeman kicked him in the face with the heel of his shoe, breaking one of Ha Hak's teeth. Afterward, they chained him outside in a metal barrel placed in the ground. It was very hot, and he had only one glass of water and a small bowl of rice each day. He wore only short pants and no shirt. At night in the highland region, the weather gets very cold.

Pastor Ha Hak (left) and Pastor Hoang Van Phung (right) are visited in prison by their wives

He was held in that barrel for three months. During that time, Pastor Ha Hak prayed and asked the Lord to help him. The Lord gave him strength. He saw a light in heaven shine on him, like the Apostle Paul on the road to Damascus (Acts 9). The Lord gave him new strength so he could get through this.

Very large snakes crawled through the holes in the barrel and slid over his feet. Since his hands and feet were chained, he couldn't do anything except pray as he watched the snakes. The Lord delivered him, and not one of the snakes bit him.

The police told me that I would be in prison for 27 years, but the Lord brought me out after only two and a half years. Today I am in charge of a mission team. I am very thankful to the Lord, because He has used many American Christians to help believers in Vietnam. I thank the servants of God in America who have been praying for us here. The Lord uses you to deliver us out of prison. I pray the Lord will bless the servants of God in America. In the name of Jesus, I love you and your country from my heart.

I pray for America and know that God blesses America because there are so many missionaries and good Christians who come from there to bless other countries. I know that there are many problems in America, but I am confident that God will continue to use many new generations of Christians to keep the foundation of the kingdom of God solid in your country.

CHAPTER 7

Standing on a Firm Foundation

That Your Joy May Be Full

My family was raised worshipping idols. We sought the counsel of witch doctors while one of my children was dying of a sickness and my wife also did not have good health and died.

After I believed in the Lord, He showed me John 16:24 in His Word, which says, "Until now you have asked nothing in My name. Ask, and you will receive, that your joy may be full." I prayed for three nights and read through the book of John.

One of my children had malaria. I prayed for healing, and on the third day my child was healed. The Lord also healed my other two children, a son and a daughter. He used these things to show me that He was real.

There was a very big meeting with 300 tribal members at the home of Brother E. His home has a bamboo floor and the roof is thatched. The walls are also bamboo tied together. We have to climb up a piece of wood, like a ladder, to the house.

Dieu Liem

Poles were placed under it to hold it up. The house is small, with three rooms. One family member lives on one side, and in the middle is a place for meeting, praying, and singing. On the other side is a room for the brothers to sleep. Many people surrounded the home during the meeting, because there was not enough room inside.

Three years ago there were only three Christian workers. But at this meeting, there were about 30 Christian workers among the group. The whole village is Christian, so they were all coming one by one to sing. The Christian workers were meeting in the upper room along with as many other Christians as would fit in the room; 100 or more had to stay outside in the yard below.

They sang and prayed loudly, so the police came. The village police wore plain clothes. As they climbed up the stairs and entered the room, the Christians did not run but kept singing.

The police brought the 30 workers to the police station, while the whole village followed them. All 300 people, including children, walked on the dirt road one and a half kilometers to the police station; only the elderly stayed at home. It looked like a big parade! We sang children's songs such as, "When I go to heaven, where the young sheep live together with beloved Jesus." When we arrived at the police station, everybody kept singing and praying. We stood outside of the building, which had a metal roof and wooden walls.

Three policemen were in the building. The police said, "This is a working place; you are not allowed to do that." But we kept singing and praying. The chief of the village told the brothers and sisters to go home.

But the whole village had followed, wanting to protect Brother E. "We need Brother E, we want Brother E." The people continued to stay. "If you want to arrest someone, arrest all of us. If you want to kill, kill all of us." The district police also came.

The district police prohibit worshipping and meeting together. Yet all 300 villagers were not afraid to ask them to release these Christian workers.

A Hunger for the Word
Many tribal people are becoming believers and want to have freedom to worship the Lord. Some haven't been taught much in the Word. The government tries to keep the tribal people very simple. One night the police brought a film into the village showing a robber who steals things; in the film, the government kills the robber. The police were using this to brainwash them.

The film also communicated a threat to pressure them: "If you do something wrong, you will be killed like this." In the picture, it was very terrifying how the government kills those

The police brought 30 workers to the police station. The whole village followed them.

who create problems. That night, the police also tried to find the source of all Christian literature to punish the one who was bringing the Bibles here.

The police asked everyone in the district one by one, "Who brought you this?" They ordered people to tell them who brought the gospel, so they could find the source.

One brother from the S'tieng tribe was the first one who had a Bible in the village. During that time, he was very terrified and not knowing much in the Word, hanged himself.

Later the police arrested Brother E again. To prevent others from following him, they "invited him" to a meeting with the village officer. They arrested him there so that the others did not see them take him away.

Brother E had two Bibles. Before he was imprisoned, he gave one to me. The police accused Brother E of forcing people to sell their buffalo or oxen, and other criminal activities. They sentenced him to three months in prison at Tong Le Chan. He sawed logs and planted white potatoes in the labor camp. His wife was allowed to see him only once.

The church was very young and they did not know how to pray, so they seldom prayed for him. When they believed in Jesus, they didn't have any Bibles, only small excerpts of Scripture. But these Scriptures were enough to give them a foundation to resist fearing persecution.

We continued to train others in the Lord to become strong and to not forsake Him. The gospel has spread from Binh Long to Phuoc Long Province, a large province. There, another brother, Tu, also believed in the Lord.

In one village, a mother who was a Christian held her dead baby in her hands. She said, "God can heal even though there is no more breath in the child." The baby was dead for half an hour and then came back to life.

I stayed at this village for a while before going to Phuoc Long Province where I helped the new converts in Christ burn all of their idols and charms. In the tribes, witch doctors are in charge of everything.

The next time I went there, 200 people gathered in the morning for a meeting. They had heard about the one-year-old baby who had come back to life. That was a divine opportunity to share the Word.

One person was bitten on the heel by a brown, poisonous snake. When someone is bitten by this kind of snake, he dies within 24 hours. There was no medical help nearby, so we prayed for this man and he lived. Some of the people in that village were disturbed by our prayers to God and this demonstration of His power, so they reported us to the police.

A Visit By the Police

Our church meeting lasted until noon. When I had finished preaching, five policemen came wearing army clothes. They had rifles and were riding motorbikes. They looked at me and said, "Not this person."

Not knowing that I was the leader, they left. If I wanted to, I could have run away. But if I had run away, I would have contradicted my teaching and left the brothers and sisters confused. If we serve the Lord, we embrace and do whatever happens to us. So I stayed there.

My Bible is the only one in the whole village, and it is very precious. There are two workers, but only one Bible—Old and New Testaments. Whatever happens, we cannot afford to lose the Bible, so we try to find ways to keep it safe.

On another occasion, I had already given my Bible to someone when I was surrounded by the police. They grabbed me by the shirt and asked, "Are you the pastor?"

I replied, "I am not a pastor."

They asked, "Are you a preacher?"

I did not know what to say. I am a simple witness for the Lord. Preacher means you are the one who shares the Word. I said, "Yes."

They tried to find evidence. They searched and searched and found a Gospel of John on another worker. They also took away one small Bible, as one had a small New Testament in his pocket.

There were many times when the police had wanted to arrest me, but they wanted to know for sure who was the one who preaches the Word. This time they knew for sure. They took me away on their motorcycle, with me sitting between them. They held guns up to me and brought me to the police station, which was quite small—two rooms about 15 meters long. There were more policemen inside the office.

The policemen questioned me about where I got the small Bible. It was not my Bible, but another worker's Bible. I said, "This Bible was from the official church."

They asked me, "Who told you to go and spread the Word like this?"

I said, "No one told me. Our villagers, our people, used to drink and gamble and do many bad things. But now we know the Word and it makes us good people, so I want to share this Word with my people."

They asked, "Where did you get this religion? Who told you to go and share this religion?"

To protect the others, I made up a story so they wouldn't know about the church. I said, "I cut up a log and floated it along the river so that I could go out to a more civilized area. Floating on the river, I went to the market areas. I saw my own people walking to an area and asked where they were going. They said they were going to a church, so I joined them. That is how I learned about this religion. I was going to sell the log at the market.

"I used to smoke, drink, and curse, but when I heard the Word, it changed me and I no longer curse, drink, or smoke." I shared with them how the Word changed me. That is why they wanted to listen to me.

They said, "What do you preach?"

I told them, "We sing like this and we pray." I began singing a song for the police, "Love Jesus day and night. Love Him more and more."

I didn't finish the song—one policeman hit me. Then they invited me to smoke; they were testing me.

I told them I didn't smoke.

The chief gave me some cigarettes from his pocket. He put one right in front of my face on the table and said, "Smoke."

I said, "I don't smoke."

Then the police took out his pistol and threatened to shoot me if I didn't smoke. Although I was the only preacher in this area, I wasn't afraid.

Afterwards they gave me some noodles. I did not eat because I wanted to fast and pray.

They told me to sing again. I sang again, the whole song, very joyfully.

That night they gave me a mat, and I slept on the dirt floor. A policeman guarded me inside the room. It was not a prison, it was the office of the police. I had no blanket to keep warm but, by His grace, I slept anyway. That night I thought about how the Lord knows the number of hairs on my head.

This was the first time I had been arrested, so I did not know what to expect. I did not think of my wife or children or anything. From seven to nine o'clock in the morning, they asked me to build a fence for the police station. They drank wine while I worked, so they could have more courage. They got drunk.

Later on they beat me and questioned me again. I just answered the same things as yesterday. Before they would beat me, they would ask me to sing. When they beat me like this it made me sweat, but I felt very healthy and strong. I was singing, "Love Jesus day and night."

When the chief of the police hit me, I prayed for the blood of Jesus to cover me. Even though I felt pain when he hit me, I said, "Praise the Lord."

The chief of police backed off and said that something had just pushed him away.

There were two more Christian workers—Brother Tu and Brother Duong—who were also being beaten. The police took turns. They focused on beating me the most, and the others just a little bit. They said I was "the president, the chairman." The beatings lasted nearly two hours. When they beat me, the other two Christians would pray.

The police would take off their hats to beat me. I saw them perspiring, very red and also shaky. They seemed afraid. They said that I had kung fu or something.

The Vietnamese police said, "You are the one who goes against our ancestor religion." When we believed in Jesus, we no longer practiced ancestor worship and no longer gave food to the ancestors. "You are the one against our morals, against our ethics." They say their ideology is atheism, but really they are ancestor worshippers. If I were a Buddhist, they would not have beat me.

One policeman behind Brother Tu kicked him in the head and Brother Tu nearly fell. These other two Christians were forced to sing also.

Now the officers said as they stopped to eat bread, "You pray so that your God will give you a charm." I said I did not feel like eating. The police ate the inside of the bread and gave me the crust. I said I still didn't feel like eating. The others were given food more politely. But not me; they continued to insult me.

About three o'clock in the afternoon, they took me to the provincial police, but they did not take the other two. Three policemen with guns were with me. I sat in the back of their jeep, chained. This is a special jeep in which they carry the criminal in the back of a cage.

The police station they took me to was bigger, a criminal prison, in Phuoc Long 30 kilometers away. When we got there, they said I had already eaten although I had not had anything. I was in no pain at all.

When the two brothers, Brother Tu and Brother Duong, returned to the village, the people asked, "How is Brother Liem? Did you see how he got hurt?"

The brothers said, "No, he didn't get hurt. He looked very healthy when he got into the jeep." They went back and told my wife. My wife also laughed with joy. She praised and thanked the Lord, and continued to pray.

These district police are more polite than the community police. The village police told them I sang, so the district police required me to sing. They asked me, "Why do you always report the same thing?"

I said that I only knew one thing, the gospel, and so there was nothing else to tell.

They took me to a prison cell. There were only two holes in the wall for air to come in and out. It was very dark inside. The door was metal with a window flap in it.

There were four prisoners inside that cell, and I was the fifth person. The old prisoners all had shaven heads. Since I was a newcomer, they tormented me and tried to trick me. They made me take off my coat, shirt, and pants. They had only short pants. They were in prison for stealing and murdering. Their ankles were chained but they were not chained to the wall.

I talked to these prisoners about Jesus.

One asked, "Are you better than us because you have hair and we are all shaved?"

I replied, "No, I am worse than you. I have a very heavy crime."

They asked what my crime was.

I said, "Preaching the gospel."

They asked what religion I was preaching. I told them I was spreading the gospel. The gospel is to believe in the Lord Jesus. Believe in Jesus and you will be changed.

They asked me if I wanted to smoke. I said, "I don't smoke because I believe in Jesus." I shared how the Lord protected me when the five policemen beat me, that they stopped beating me because they got sick right there.

When we received food, we each had a bowl of rice, half a handful of salt, and a bowl of soup, mainly water. I said, "Let us pray so that the Lord can free us." I closed my eyes and prayed. I don't know whether they closed their eyes or not. Then I ate only three or four spoonfuls and gave the rest to them because they looked terribly thin.

I gave rice to one man; the other three men did not eat my portion. They looked at me and saw that I was also skinny. They were afraid I would die, so they wouldn't take it from me. I said, "I am all right. I am strong." But they still didn't take my portion.

The next morning I was called for more questioning. When they finished their report, they released me.

My wife was planning to borrow some money to buy some food to visit me, because we didn't have any money. But then she saw me coming joyfully down the road. The whole village rejoiced! I ran right into my home. The people in the village came and asked me how I was.

I told them that the Lord did a miracle. They listened and were very touched.

The Christians in the Phuoc Long area also asked me, "Are you okay?" I told them that when the police beat me, they wanted to dislocate a rib but nothing happened.

I have continued to preach until now. My favorite Bible verse is Galatians 2:20, "I have been crucified with Christ; it is no longer I who live, but Christ lives in me."

CHAPTER 8

A Pastor's Wife

Preparing for Persecution

Before 1975 my friends and I did not know how the Communists in Vietnam would begin to treat the people. But since we read the book *Tortured for Christ*, we realized that in a Communist country people cannot freely worship. We knew that we had to prepare ourselves.

Two days after the fall of Saigon to the Communists in April 1975, I was in a student meeting with Pastor Cuong. He had been trained in the U.S. with the Christian Missionary Alliance. He had come back to Vietnam and was willing to stay, even though he was later sent to prison for many years. Pastor Cuong also had read *Tortured for Christ*, so he knew that if the other pastors were arrested and the churches were closed, then the Christians could still stand on their feet, teach one another, and study the Bible together. Pastor Cuong was taking care of the student work by preparing us to keep the faith under the Communist regime.

Mrs. Nguyen

We met in a former evangelical Christian bookstore. The students had to form teams—three teams with three Christians in each. Pastor Cuong chose me to be in the first group, which meant that we would later train in other provinces.

During that time, I worked in an Every Home for Christ crusade program and at a Far East Broadcasting station. Pastor Nguyen, my future husband, would come to the crusade and preach. I was 22 and he was 23. I didn't really know him. Pastor Cuong invited Pastor Nguyen to join a student committee.

My homeland is in Phan Rang on the countryside in north central Vietnam. I was assigned to go to Phan Rang to share with the churches in three provinces. Since we were already aware that churches would be closed under Communist governments, we prepared Christians to meet in their homes for when this would occur in our country (which was in 1975).

During the time I stayed in Phan Rang, Pastor Nguyen had to go back to the Bible school in Nha Trang to finish one more year. Nha Trang is about 100 kilometers from my home. We wrote back and forth. Once in a while, he asked the ministry for permission to go from Nha Trang to Phan Rang to help with the work in our area.

After 1975, the government began to arrest pastors. The government asked every pastor to register the hour they planned to have a meeting. We could have a worship meeting on Sunday for only one hour. All the rest of the activities were forbidden—no more children's ministry under 18 and no more Sunday school.

I invited many other young people to come to the place where I started to train them about how to work as a "3–3 team." [*Editor's note:* This refers to three people on a team, with three teams each focusing on a different aspect of ministry: evangelism, training, or pastoring.] Many pastors and Christians were afraid of the Communists. In some places, Christians even renounced their faith. I had to choose the trustworthy students because if they were not trustworthy, they would spy on us and report to the police.

I also traveled to other places to train. A person who wants to go from one part of the country to another is required to have government permission or have some relatives to visit. I signed a paper stating that I wanted to visit my relatives, and the government allowed me to go. Sometimes I went even if I did not have any relatives to visit. We would study at night, because in the daytime we had to work. When we would hear dogs barking, we thought the police were checking the houses. Christians who were bold would let me stay with them. We would keep our study groups limited to three people, because we were not allowed to meet in big groups. If three people met together, it looked like an informal visit.

A Perfect Union

In 1977, Pastor Nguyen and I were married. A choir of young people sang at our wedding. We were not allowed to wear beautiful clothes because if anything looked expensive, we would have to pay a fine. The Communists called this a "stupid fine," because they think it is very stupid to pay the money for luxury items like a nice wedding dress. So I borrowed a simple white dress. Pastor Nguyen borrowed a gray suit.

Since my registration was in Phan Rang, I could not move to Ho Chi Minh City without permission. I was 24, and our country was at war with Cambodia. All the young people who were in school had to join the army. My wealthy family was in business, but the government had confiscated our house. My mother died and then my father was hit by an army truck.

One of my father's friends felt sorry for me. He had been a close friend, but had joined the army and gone to the North to become a Communist Party member. When he returned and saw my situation, he allowed me to work for his company. I estimated product costs by researching industrial companies and small corporations. I would check to see what kind of labor they were doing and would track the products from beginning to end to find out how much it would cost. I worked there for two years.

I finally quit my job and went to Ho Chi Minh City. I could not find a job, because my background of formerly well-to-do people and of Christians was not good in the eyes of the government. My husband, being a preacher, was "no good" also. The class system restricted us. We stayed with my husband's parents in a small room in their small house.

Since my husband was an assistant pastor of a church and had no salary, I had to work to support him. I walked all around the city from morning until evening with a small cart selling cotton candy and French bread with meat in it. I would wear black pants, a blouse, and a pointed Chinese-style "Non La" hat.

At first I was very ashamed working like this, because I came from a well-to-do family. Sometimes when I ran into my old friends, they cried. But I thought within myself that I do this because I want to support a servant of God. So I just continued this work.

I stopped at the schools when the children were at play time. The sun was very hot. I would sit down and rest a little bit. The children would come out, and I would sell to them. The little kids realized from my educated speech that I was not from a poor family, but just because of the situation of the country, I had to do this. So they would kindly call me "Miss." They would bring their notebooks to ask me something about the lesson in school, mathematics or another subject. I shared the gospel with them.

A Hunger to Preach the Word

In 1981, my husband started to hunger for the Lord very much, so he wanted to go into the wilderness to seek the Lord. In 1982, I also felt a strong hunger for the Lord. I quit selling things and started to seek the Lord for one year in 1983.

We were assigned to Truon Minh Giang church in 1984. My husband preached the message of repentance every week in the pulpit. We invited a small group of people to come together to pray for revival.

The official church publicly dismissed my husband in October 1989. Now we had two daughters. With my experience in cost estimation, I went into the big market to buy things to take to smaller markets to sell. At the same time I bought our food. A Christian sister sent a few dollars to help me, and my own sister in America also sent us some help.

When my husband was dismissed, 13 young workers left with us and continued to pray together. They were all zealous for the Lord but did not know much Scripture. Pastor Nguyen and Pastor Thuyen started to train these people, but did not send them out yet. My husband trained them for two years until October 1991 when he was arrested. In 1992 the brothers started to go out and evangelize.

Twenty-one Policemen

The day my husband was arrested, a local policeman came to talk with him at 7:00 a.m. I knew something was going to happen that day. I was upstairs and tried to hide different kinds of papers including the 20 new Bibles that I had received.

Fifteen minutes later, 20 more policemen arrived in three jeeps. They waited to read the arrest order. Some were in uniforms, some just in plain clothes. They belonged to the city police, district police, and the secretary's bureau.

About 15 policemen came inside our home while others stayed in the jeeps outside. Once they came into our home, they told Pastor Nguyen to call me downstairs. They forced him to stand in one place. One officer, a general, said, "We ask you, the wife, to listen to the arrest order for Mr. Nguyen."

I said, "What crime did my husband commit?"

He angrily shouted, "You cannot ask for proof! You must obey the government!"

So I answered, "If you talk like that, I will ask you to go out of my house right away!"

A local policemen near me said, "You cannot talk to my higher leader like this!"

I replied, "I have read in the papers many times that there are false police coming into people's homes and harassing and stealing and ripping things, so I want to know whether you are true or false. You show me your papers that prove yourself to be true policemen. Then I will work with you."

The general softened his voice and said, "This is the order from a higher authority. If you have any questions, you will go to the higher authority."

I quickly replied, "If that is so, let me see your higher authority. If needed, I will even meet with the president of Vietnam."

Pastor Nguyen patiently told me to let them read the order. One policeman read that they were arresting Pastor Nguyen to be sent away for re-education for three years. The charge was "illegally preaching the gospel."

I questioned this order, "My husband is a preacher. He preaches the gospel and he's a good citizen. He didn't commit any crime. Why don't you go and arrest the robbers, the murderers? You should know us as a benefactor of this country. You don't have any proof, any evidence, yet you can come and arrest him like this. It's no good."

Then Pastor Nguyen sat calmly and answered, "I knew that this day would come. I am ready to go."

After they finished reading the arrest order, they read a second order for checking our house.

"What do you want to look for in my home?" I demanded.

They said, "We will take whatever we need to take and find whatever we need to find."

I challenged them, "Are you taking the opportunity to steal my things? You have come into the homes of the people and taken their personal things. When you found out this person didn't commit any crime, their things were gone, destroyed."

Finally, the general said, "I promise you that we will take only what we need to investigate and question Mr. Nguyen. We won't take away any of your personal things."

I saw many stars on his shoulders and asked my husband, "Pastor Nguyen, what rank is this?"

He said, "General, three stars."

I looked around at all the other lower policemen and said, "You all listen to that. He promised not to take any personal things of mine. So I will allow you to go and check."

They all wanted to go upstairs.

I said, "No, I will allow only five to go up."

When they went upstairs, all five wanted to "check" the house. Sometimes the policemen throw something in the corner then take it out and accuse you of a crime. My two daughters were small and I was by myself, so I said, "No. I don't have many eyes, so if I look at this person, the other person can take something out of his pocket and then accuse me of something."

I saw another policeman looking in my basket, taking out a letter. The letter had names of Christian friends. I ran over, grabbed it, and threw it away. I said, "You are very impolite, reading another person's letter."

The policeman said, "You are too crabby. I am a policeman. I am doing my duty."

The Lord helped me to think quickly. So I told him, "It's not that I won't allow you, but you didn't ask my permission first. Even my husband has to ask permission."

In our home we have a lot of cassette tapes, music, and preaching tapes in a big box. The police wanted to bring them all to the office to check.

I said, "No, I have my tape recorder here. You just check it now. You cannot bring anything out."

The policemen did not take many things out of our house. It was my husband they wanted. They just took a number of his sermons and papers where we had written the history of the house church in Vietnam. Since we had written it a long time ago, I had forgotten to hide it.

We went downstairs, and the police signed for all the things they were carrying out. Pastor Nguyen said, "Now, my family has to pray before we leave."

The police permitted that. So the four of us—two children, my husband, and me—knelt down in the living room. The police waited inside the room. Our two little daughters cried and prayed, "Father, our God, give our father peace and keep his church at peace." Then I prayed, and Pastor Nguyen prayed, "Even though I go, I go in the name of Jesus. I pray that peace be upon the church and that everyone will protect it." We prayed for half an hour. We thanked the Lord that they didn't put him in handcuffs, but just let him go out in the jeep. Twenty-one policemen had come for one man.

Chalk Marks on the Wall

The police brought him to a place across from the floating hotel, the security prison and anti-spy investigation office on the Saigon River. There they isolated him for three months. During those months, I could not see his face. The police allowed me to send food once a month. The Lord moved the hearts of many brothers and sisters in the church. They kept bringing our family food and gifts, so I could take them to the prison for Pastor Nguyen. The children and I saved the best food for him. We ate simple things.

Our ten-year-old daughter had heard the sentence of three years. She was in the fifth grade and her sister was in the seventh grade when he was sent to prison. She used chalk to mark the date on the wall, November 30, 1991, noting also what year in school she would be in, and what grade her sister would be in when he should be released.

The first month our daughters dropped from good students to average students. All their marks went down. I began to encourage them. I shared about how things are like this, and they understood. They prayed for Daddy, and their studies improved again. They also did not feel inferior with their friends because their father was arrested. The youngest, Duc

Linh, said, "I want to trade places with Dad, so that he can come out."

After three months, the police allowed me to send food twice a month, and I was allowed to see him once a month for 15 minutes. Then he went to Phan Dang Luu, and they later moved him to a labor camp, Tong Le Chan.

Some of the brothers and sisters in the church went with me to visit Pastor Nguyen at the camp. We didn't know how much time we would have to meet with him. The guards were leading the prisoners out to a more remote area when Pastor Nguyen saw me with the Christians and said, "Hallelujah!" The police were very shocked. They didn't know what he said. Outside the fence our little group joyfully said, "Hallelujah!"

There was a table about one-meter long. A fence was between us, so we could only sit on our side and he sat across, far away. We could not give him anything and I was not allowed to touch him.

After asking about the family, he asked about the church. "How about my fishing pond? Is it growing and is something happening to it?" We used code words, because the guards were very touchy. The meeting was very short, only 15 minutes. Before he went back into the prison camp, he said that he had accepted his imprisonment and told us not to be concerned.

One time when I went to the prison to visit Pastor Nguyen, I tore pages of the Bible and made them into a bag, then put food inside. When he received the food, he could keep the pages that I made the bag with and read the Bible. I also sent letters wrapped in a plastic bag inside the meat. I told him that when he ate, he should be careful. He could find a letter in it.

Sometimes Pastor Nguyen sent letters that he wrote in prison in very tiny, little words and wrapped them in plastic bags. He also wrote 30 songs in prison—without a guitar or any other musical instrument. So when the police came, sometimes we put the letters and song notes in our mouth.

Christians from outside Vietnam came and said they wanted to help in this matter. I told them I wasn't afraid. I

would go to all the
higher authorities to
talk about this even
though they could
imprison me. I want
to tell this to every-
one so that those
who follow after us
will not suffer this
kind of injustice. I
want to speak up so
the world will know
about this situation
in Vietnam, so that

Christians must meet secretly to baptize new believers. Many are arrested for this "crime."

others will receive attention, not only my husband.

After meeting with my husband in prison, they allowed me to visit again for a few months. They called me to the police bureau in an isolated area and questioned me on two mornings from eight to twelve o'clock. The first morning, one policeman questioned me about the church. I advised him, "Just leave the church alone. Don't bother her, don't perse-cute her. You should know that the Roman Empire had perse-cuted the Christians greatly, but the more they persecuted, the more the church grew."

He answered, "I know, but this is our duty because you use religion and abuse it to work for a political cause."

Then he asked me, "Why did the church leadership dismiss you, yet you are still preaching the gospel?"

I said, "My ambition is to preach the gospel, and I will preach the gospel my whole life. My desire is to share the gospel with more than 60 million Vietnamese, and that in-cludes you (the officer)."

The next day, I had a chance to tell him many things about the gospel. I felt so very touched, so moved that I cried. The policeman also seemed like he wanted to cry. He said that he had a Bible, because he was in charge of religious matters. He had the revised New Testament. He also said that he had an aunt who was a Christian. He said he read the Bible because he wanted to know what to teach about.

I said, "If you want to accept, just know that I will pray for you right away." I showed him John 3:16 and John 1:12 in his Bible.

Later I met him on the road on our motorbikes. He called to me. As I looked back in traffic and saw him in his uniform driving behind me, I slowed down and we drove together. I said, "How are you? Are you at peace? Did you read the Bible?" He laughed, then drove off.

When I decided to stay in Vietnam to serve the Lord, I knew that I would be persecuted, and I was ready for it. I believed that when my husband or the other pastors were arrested, they would not be lonely because other Christians in Vietnam and in other parts of the world would be praying for them.

I also believe that if we love our children, God will love them and care for them more than we could ourselves. While I am still with the children, I will raise them up and teach them in the Word. But I will also teach them who their parents are and that they are to serve the Lord. If we are arrested, they will know that it is because of the love of God. It's not because we want to leave them.

One time, after Pastor Nguyen was arrested, I asked the children what they want to do when they grow up. The older girl said, "I want to be a missionary."

I asked, "Aren't you afraid to be arrested like your father?"

And she said, "No." Our children said they are very proud of him. The Word of God is a source of strength for our family.

I have many favorite Scriptures, but the one that I remember most and am most encouraged by like an oath, like a promise for me is, "I and my household will serve the Lord."

CHAPTER 9

The Shining One

At Gunpoint

Once some fellow workers and I crossed over to a village in Cambodia and began to pray and share the gospel. A Cambodian soldier was standing in his house with an AK rifle wanting to shoot us where we were singing and praying. The soldier's wife, who was standing with him, later told us that he hates it when people pray. But she told him, "If they want to pray, just let them pray. Don't shoot them." He didn't shoot.

I have traveled a long way and have seen many miracles happen. This is just one of them. This is how it began...

I was the first in my village, Phuoc Tien, to become a Christian. I was working in the People's Council when I received Christ. Someone found out about this and called the police. I was imprisoned. The police said, "You are a member of the People's Council, but you also preach the gospel. That's not allowed." But later I preached the Word anyway. My whole village has come to Jesus —first my relatives, then neighbors, and then the whole village.

One day I became sick and went to the provincial hospital in

Dieu Dung

Ben Yu for treatment. I had to pay one bar of gold (equal to nearly $500 U.S. and over a year's income in Vietnam). That's very big money for a tribal person, but I was not cured.

They said that my lungs and heart were very bad, even after treatment. I received all kinds of injections and had an operation. I didn't know much about the Word, but I prayed and the Lord healed me.

After this happened, I visited one of my cousins. He was also sick and was in much pain. He had paid one ring of gold (about $50 U.S.), but was not well. I shared my testimony. I didn't know much about *how* to share but I did it anyway. That was the first time I shared the gospel after accepting Christ.

Soon after, I went down to Min and received a Bible. Every afternoon I would go to encourage everyone, sharing the Word, and holding meetings in my house.

My first wife died. I have only one child from her. Now I have another wife and four more children. We are very poor. I plant rice, and we have a buffalo for plowing. We dug a well ten meters in front of our house down a slope, where I go for the water.

We have a thatched-roof house with two rooms. We don't have anything on the walls like pictures. Everybody crowds into those rooms. We have no electricity, but use a kerosene lantern. We put the lantern on the table, and everybody sits on the dirt floor so we can see.

Whenever we pray, we close the door. The police have threatened to arrest us many times, but whenever we sing, we still sing loudly. We know many songs from the official church, and we have learned many other songs from house church groups. We don't have much food, but the Christians buy cookies and candies and bring them to the meetings.

Opposition from the Authorities

At first we had only one group of 20 people at my house. Now with so many, we divide into four groups in four houses. Thursday is fasting and prayer day. Every Sunday at 7:30 or 8:00 in the morning we come together.

There are village police, district police, and border police in different sections of our village. Whenever I share and sing in villages, the police usually call me to the office about gathering the people to preach the gospel.

The first time I was in jail, I was a new Christian and did not tell the police about Jesus. I had not read the Bible much and was afraid. They let me see my wife briefly and receive some food. During that five minutes, I told her, "Be at peace, this is no problem." She remained quiet.

I knew of Christians from the official church who had been arrested already. But after I read the Bible, I was not afraid when I was imprisoned again.

My younger brother lives in another house in the same village. He was arrested one week earlier for preaching the gospel. Two other relatives were arrested also.

Since then, the police have brought me to the police office many times, using a book to beat and slap me. I would sit in the room for one or two hours. Four or five times, they said I must write that I violated the law of Decree 69.

Decree 69 means that we have the freedom to worship only at home, but the government interprets it in a different way. They wanted me to say that I am anti-government and that I gather the people illegally to preach. I said, "The people gather in my home, and I pray and share what I know in the Word with them. I don't do anything outside of that."

One time the district police put me in a jeep. They were all drunk and grabbed me by the ear. They said, "You stupid fool, going to preach the Word," and they hit me on the head. I thought, "The Lord is allowing me to go to prison." We went more than 30 kilometers to the district where they put me in prison. This six-room jail is in Loc Ninh.

I stayed there 11 days. I praised the Lord for why I was in prison. I witnessed and one prisoner became a Christian.

The police took me out to ask me questions. While I sat in a chair, they sat in front of me at a wooden table and screamed at me. They had confiscated two Bibles and some hymn books from other villages and put them in a closet. They kept using a Bible and hymn book to hit my forehead. I did not have an official trial. At times after the police had interrogated me for a while, they would run out of questions.

They pushed me into a cell and locked the door. There was no window, so it was dark in the cell. Five other prisoners were lying on the cement floor. We had a bucket for a toilet, and the room smelled terrible.

Bibles are given to Dieu Dung

The five prisoners were robbers. They wanted to hit me. Usually the old prisoners threaten and try to oppress the new ones.

Pointing to one of the prisoners, the jailer told me, "This man has a chain. He is a robber." The robber was about 27 years old, tall with a long face and a foreign look. He had tattoos of men on his chest. He had long hair and was from the North. The robber's feet were still chained. He was the only one chained. He looked like a cruel person, wanting to beat me.

My wife had given me a few bags of noodles, so I gave the other prisoners the rice. If I prayed out loud, they would beat me. After I fasted and prayed within my heart for two days, they were nice to me. They moved near me and one asked, "I hear that you sing well. Will you sing?"

Each night I would sing praises. One of the songs was, "When we look at the cross, we meditate on Jesus." They didn't know how to sing so they listened. They said, "Oh, very nice."

Two nights in a row, I was sleeping when the robber in chains saw a beautiful person in white come to visit me. Only the robber saw this vision. He asked, "Who are you?"

This person in white said, "I have come to visit him," pointing at me.

Still amazed, the robber said again, "Who are you, where are you going?"

Again the shining one said, "I came to visit this person." The shining person walked over to me.

The robber told me in the morning, "If you can pray for me so that I can be released from this chain, I will believe."

I said, "You receive the Lord into your heart and go back home. Don't do these bad things, don't rob again, and the Lord will bless you." I laid my hand on the poor robber and prayed for him to receive Jesus. I shared with all of them Romans 3:23, Romans 3:16,17, and John 1:12.

The next morning I was released. The police brought me back home on a Honda motorbike. I heard a day later that the robber had his chains taken off.

The authorities had gathered all the people—about 300—in my village school. They had been waiting for the police to bring me back. When I got off the Honda at my house, the whole village, which is now Christian, ran out of the school to the motorbike. As I walked into the school, they shouted with joy. A revival began to break out in my village as we shared.

The police stood at a table, reading their legal papers while the people were shaking my hand and hugging me. The police read an announcement that I had violated the law, and how many times I had violated it by preaching the Word. They said I must promise to do this no longer.

The villagers said that they would support me if later on I "violated laws" and was arrested. They did not care that the policeman was listening.

Last week the police came to my house. At that time, the whole church was meeting in our home. The police pointed at me and said, "You have violated the law many times, and you intend to continue. We will arrest you."

But then the believers there told them, "You just sit here and see what we will do. We will pray, and after we pray we will leave. We won't do anything."

The Lord at Work

In my area the Lord is continuing to heal many people who cannot speak, are demon-possessed, and have other problems. Our tribe has relatives in Cambodia, and we visit there frequently. They call us and say, "Tell Brother Dieu to come visit. We want to receive Jesus."

But in my village, no one wants to go. Then the Holy Spirit makes one of us so burdened inside that we pray, ask the Lord, and then go, crossing a big forest.

Many Christian workers do not have Bibles. When we take Bibles into Cambodia, we have to wrap them in clothes. Sometimes our Bibles are confiscated by the Vietnamese border guards.

Many times when I went out to evangelize, I faced many difficulties at home. No one would help my family while I was gone, so sometimes I wanted to stop evangelizing. But I am the "leading bird in the whole flock," so if I am weak, then how will the flock be? One night I prayed, and the Lord spoke to me in a dream and gave me Matthew 5:3, "Blessed are the poor in spirit, for theirs is the kingdom of heaven." That made me content and joyful to go.

The work here is just beginning, and "Caesar" (the government) wants to cause much persecution to hinder the work. My two brothers work with the children's ministry. Now more people want to go. I ask brothers and sisters around the world to pray for the Bu Dop area so that the church here will become very strong and be a center for many brothers and sisters to come and be trained, so that the work will spread out.

A Christian blind man from this area feels his way at night along the dirt trail into Cambodia. He does not need light. He is one of the best witnesses for Christ.

If others around the world pray, it is like a hen and her little chicks. When there is no mother, then the wolf can come and eat them. But when there is a mother over them, then the wolf dares not come.

I will finish by singing a song for you...

He sings praises

CHAPTER 10

Isolated Yet Free

Fourteen Years of Exile

Many years ago, the leadership of the Christian Missionary Alliance (CMA) appointed me and my family to stay in our large church building in the city of Can Tho. After the Communist takeover, the police came with guns to confiscate the church. But I would not hand over God's property. I told them that I was only the manager, not the owner, so I could not give over this building. If they want to take it, they must sign a paper from a higher Authority.

"Then we'll shoot you," they threatened.

A Communist Party member declared himself pastor of the church, and the authorities placed my family and me under house arrest. In April 1982, the policemen took me, my wife, and our ten children in a van to an empty house in a remote area 50 kilometers from the capital in the Mekong delta. They isolated us like this because I was the leader of the southern area for the Evangelical Church of Vietnam. Many other pastors were under my supervision.

When the Communists first took over, they said that the policy of the last regime was not right, and pastors were not allowed to join the government then.

Pastor Lap Ma and his wife

85

But now, the Communist government promotes its "true policy": all pastors must join the Party. Buddhists and all classes of people also must join. If they do not, the authorities say they are anti-government. They used me as an example to persuade other pastors. They isolated me, so that I would not use my high authority to influence other pastors to not work with the government.

The government demanded that I join the "National Front" of the Party. To do so, I would become a politician and have to say things for the government. I refused, because I am not a politician. I am a pastor.

The government also asked other pastors under me to join this organization and report the activities of their church, such as who are the strongest Christians, who is sharing the gospel, and who is going to the army. Pastors who are sharing the gospel outside the official church do not join this front.

They treated us worse than if we had been in prison. Only one person goes to prison, but my whole family was forced to be under house arrest as an example to other pastors. The police also took away all of our clothes, our letters, our books, and other property. They would only allow my family to move in and out of an area one kilometer by three kilometers.

The children are allowed to go to school, but they have to come back to the house each day. One of my children is good in mathematics but was not allowed to enter a special school to develop his ability. Another one of my children was not able to enter college because school authorities never processed his paperwork. My children were refused special awards and were not eligible to receive financial aid.

Our children registered in school by using a different home address, so for a while three of them were not in captivity with the rest of the family.

My neighbors are not controlled like this. When my children go to school, the officers write to school officials that I am "a pastor and have violated the laws and committed political crimes." But I have given my life to serve the Lord and don't require anything. Like Job said, "If the Lord kills me, I will still trust Him."

When we were still in exile at Long My in 1982, 28 CMA pastors in our area of southern Vietnam and the leader of our denomination wrote a protest letter, asking them to release me. But the pastor in charge of my old church filed papers to further accuse me and forced people to sign these papers against their will. For many years God convicted this pastor, had mercy on him, and waited for his repentance. He never repented. But soon he had to leave the church, then the congregation grew to over 100 and the moral standard of the community improved greatly.

A Christian girl was arrested for three months because she supported me. All those who had signed the letter protesting my arrest were called to the police and were harassed by them.

We lived in this first place of isolation, AP Four, for nine and a half years. We were not allowed to build any relationships with people. The police would not allow me to do pastoral care for anyone. If I wanted to go someplace, I had to fill out an application and give it to the police, telling where I wanted to go and what I wanted to do there. If I wanted a visitor, he had to follow the same procedure.

Many people came to know the Lord while we lived at AP Four. That's why the police moved us to another place, AP Six, where more than 40 people came to know the Lord. We have been in this tiny place for three years and have been in exile for a total of 12 years.

Breaking Their Own Laws

According to regulation 29 of Vietnamese law, "A period for house arrest is one to five years after the date of conviction." The law also says, "No one is considered guilty unless tried by a court and found to be guilty." Since I have never appeared in court to be convicted of any crime, I am not a criminal. Yet I am considered guilty and punished without a court hearing.

In this obscure place, the law of the land has no meaning and can be anything they make it to be.

The authorities say that if I am quiet and obey the government, no problems will happen to me. But since I keep preaching the gospel, they keep causing problems for us. They disguise things, so when officials or others from around the world ask about my case, they can lie and say, "Oh, he's free. He's in the field. He can go fishing. He can plant rice. He can do anything."

Another reason they want to keep our whole family isolated is because they know that my wife is also a preacher. She can do many things like me, so they also stop her and all ten children who give their lives to preach the gospel and serve the Lord as well.

For a time, we had no food. Out of desperation, my wife risked her life by renting a small stand in the marketplace to sew and earn money for food. But soon the authorities forbid her to conduct business, charging that "Mrs. Lap Ma is guilty of assembling people to preach the gospel." This was not true, so she appealed to the authorities. But they came and tore down her stand. The Lord, however, led her to a goodhearted person who let her sew in a secluded place.

One of our married daughters, Nguyen Thi Kim Thanh, who is 28, has to live with us. Once in a while she asks permission to go back to visit her husband, who lives in another village. With police permission, her husband will come to visit her once in a while.

A Voice for God's People
If this problem of exile was only for me, I would be silent. But I think of the future of many Vietnamese who do not know the Lord. And in my old church, the flock is half dead because of a government pastor. Many people need to be saved and receive Jesus. I can read and write English. I could translate a printed sermon. So last March, I signed an application asking the government to bring me to court.

The Communists say one thing and do another. If the brothers from other countries question them about my case, they say, "Oh, we treat him kindly; he has freedom." But ask them to show you the order that I have been dismissed out of my home and out of captivity. Write to the Vietnamese president about my case. Tell him where I live, or the authorities will deny our problems.

After so many long years, our situation is finally known. We are not forgotten. We appreciate all the brothers and sisters who have prayed and supported and helped us to continue serving the Lord. We ask for prayer continually, so the Lord will give us the grace and the strength to be peaceful like the prophet Elijah and John the Baptist. Even though these men were strong, many times they were also discouraged. Pray for me and my family that we will be full of strength to be faithful until death.

We have endured for a long time. Even in the years of great trial and persecution when I thought our children would get discouraged and not serve the Lord, all of them kept their love for Him. Except for two children still going to school, the other eight are grown. I am training them to be servants of God. All of them are serving the Lord full-time.

Since we have been receiving hundreds of letters, the authorities have been very angry; they get infuriated about these letters. I suggest that foreigners come right to the place where we live and talk to the Christians here. The best thing is to meet with the authorities face-to-face about my case.

Since you have publicized our case to the world, our three children who had registered elsewhere can come back and visit once a week to study the Bible with us. The police don't say anything, so we are bold and continue studying our Bible together. When we were first put under house arrest, we did not have permission to go to Ho Chi Minh City. But now we can if we complete an application and have it approved by the police.

My desire, my hunger, is to be free to preach the gospel. My life is in the Lord's hands. The apostle Paul said that his life was in the Lord's hands, but sometimes Paul also appealed to Caesar to answer his case. I pray that through you, attention will be placed on my case. Please write to us:

Pastor Nguyen Lap Ma
Ap 6, Thi Tran Long My
Huyen Long My
Tinh Can-Tho
Vietnam

CHAPTER 11

The One Whom We Fear

A Prepared Heart

My favorite Bible verse is Matthew 10:28, which says, "Do not fear those who kill the body but cannot kill the soul. But rather fear Him who is able to destroy both soul and body in hell." Therefore, while we are under persecution, we know the One we must fear—God, not man. This verse became real to me when I was faced with the question of whether I was to fear God or man. This is how it started.

Nearly 1,000 people live in my village, and only ten families are Christians. Although they became Christians before I did and are older than I am, I faced arrest and persecution first.

A sister in Christ enjoyed singing her favorite songs, "Who is He? Who is He? Who is the Lord? Who is He that everyone sings of Him? Who is He that everybody loves Him?" and "If there are times you feel your heart is troubled, if there are times you feel you're lonely, look up..."

She told me, "Why don't you go to church? You love the Lord very much. Just pray to the Lord tonight and ask Him to forgive you of all your sins, and then come to our place."

K'Thien

That night, while I walked from one end of the village to the other, I was in doubt. I knew I was so full of sin. I thought, *Maybe the Lord will not visit me.*

Then that night I met with the others in a home. I felt His presence and said, "Only two more minutes." Then the Lord visited me. I felt very funny during that time.

Two girls from the city who came to the meeting asked me, "Did you pray much? Did you prepare your heart last night?"

I answered in my simple faith, "Yes, I prayed the Lord's Prayer the whole night, so I was well-prepared." It was all that I knew at that time.

They answered, "It's wonderful that the Lord only looks into the heart."

This was a turning point for my life and my family. Since then, I have received great strength from the Lord.

My sister gave me a New Testament, and I read the whole thing on the road back home. When I would leave my house, I would hide it at the head of my bed. At that time, I had two children. One night, I began to lay hands on my children, praying for them.

Facing Opposition

I started to experience persecution first from my husband. Even though he had forsaken the Communist Party, he was still full of atheism. He often came home drunk late at night. I started to fear that he would beat me. I would try to find a way to lay hands on him and pray for him. One day a fly landed right on his shoulder, so I took a chance to put my hand on his shoulder as if to scare the fly. It worked, so I prayed for him. Since then, he has been much kinder to me.

One Sunday morning at one of our meetings, a Christian worker came to share the Word, but she was pregnant and tired. She asked me, "Will you share for me?"

Every day when I read the Bible, I write down in a notebook what the Lord has taught me, so I shared in James 3 that faith must have works. I opened my notebook while sharing with 26 men, women, and children.

Suddenly, two police came. Everybody stopped. While I was kneeling down to hide the Bible under the cloth of my sarong, I saw two pairs of blue trousers—the police—under the crack of the door. I had enough time to hide my Bible, but not my notebook. They burst in and said, "Don't move!" While questioning us, the police said to me, "You speak very clearly." I speak clearly because I teach kindergarten.

When they looked at my notebook, they thought it was from someone in the city who wrote sermons for us, because the clear handwriting did not look like that of a tribal person. They asked, "Are you the chief of this group?"

I replied simply that it was an honor for me to have the opportunity to share that day. I was a Christian worker in the church and also the treasurer.

But then they said, "You are the chief of the group, so you must write down the names of everybody here."

I wrote down the names of everyone, and they compared my notebook with this list of names and saw the similar handwriting. They no longer questioned me about the notebook.

That was Sunday, so they did not arrest me right away. But they said that tomorrow they would take me and the owner of this house to the district police.

Monday came. I didn't know that they would put me in a dark room for three days and three nights. It was a small room with a rotten straw mat, very terrible. They called me to the office each morning at seven and questioned me until noon. Then they took me back to the cell. They called me again to the office at two o'clock in the afternoon, then returned me to the cell at five.

This was my first time in prison because of the Lord. I sang
songs such as, "Jesus, the good Shepherd, come to speak to the
scattered sheep." I said, "Praise the Lord!"

The Hole in the Wall

When I prayed, the Lord told me to witness to the others
around me. I looked around and said, "Nobody is here." I kept
looking, then I saw a place where the rotten mat was when I
first came in. I pushed it aside from the wall and saw a small
hole. It was difficult to see much, as it was so small. I got on my
stomach and looked through that hole and saw people from
North Vietnam in the other room. There were six men, some
were boys. I called to them, "Why are you here?"

They told me that they were drunk and beat one another.
They shared their stories. "We saw you walk out of the police
office. You are a nice girl," they said. "But what crime did you
commit that you are here?"

I saw a young boy about 20 years old. First, I listened to his
voice, but could not see his whole face. When I shared about
the gospel, he cried. I gave him my address and said, "When-

I pushed the rotten mat aside and looked through the hole.

ever you are released, come to my house, and I will give you
some money to go back to the North."

When the police opened the door, we had to use something to hide the hole. There was a hall in the middle of the
prison. There were four rooms on one side and four rooms on
the other side. The wall was cement, but the doors were wood.
There was a crack in the door. Whenever they would unlock
the first door, which has an iron bar (I was in the second
room), I had time to hide the hole.

I talked to the boys and men for three days. The young
men often called to me through the hole, and I prayed for
them. They said, "What are you doing? Do you miss your
home? Do you miss your children?"

I have three children. The first is a daughter, the second a
son, and the third a daughter, four years old. While I was
talking with them, I had a strong desire to see my youngest
daughter. My husband brought her to visit, but the Lord
helped my child not to cry or run to me. She just enjoyed
looking at the different pictures that the police showed her.

The police taunted me, "See, even your child sees that you
commit sin, so she doesn't look at you."

I was not afraid of the police, but I was afraid for my
husband, because he got very angry. He told the police,
"There are many worse people robbing. Why don't you arrest
them? My wife didn't do anything wrong. Why did you arrest
her? If the whole village would be as good as my wife, there
would be no problems, so why did you arrest her?"

The two older children knew I had been arrested, but my
youngest one said, "Where did you go that you didn't sleep
with me for three nights?"

The day that I was released, there was only one motorbike,
so my brother and my husband came to bring me home. My
husband waited at the market on the bicycle with my little one.
When my brother drove me to the market, the little one saw
me and clung to me, not allowing me to go anywhere. But the
police were not finished with me.

The police fined me 500,000 dong. They brought me in front of the whole village to accuse and humiliate me. At first, they tried to be polite with me by using emotional words. Then after a while, they started to yell at me, pushing and bumping the table in the open village hearing. They said, "You are a child of God, so you always tell the truth. You will not tell lies, because if you tell lies you will not only commit crimes with the government, but also commit sins with God."

The district police hate those who pray in tongues. They found out about tongues by reading the Bible and papers from a church. They called me a worker of Pentecostals. They put my story on the television and in the newspaper to ridicule me. This was in May 1994, in the province of Lam Dong, the community of Duy Linh.

The TV station in Duy Linh asked me to write my story. I wrote three pages about preaching the gospel. They told me to write that I think speaking in tongues causes one to be stupid. Many people who don't know Jesus would read this kind of article.

Three weeks later, the police put me in a jeep and brought me to a village. I was forced to write that I would never preach again. They asked me to read this in front of people, and then they videotaped me. The police said, "You will violate the law if you preach the gospel in another house, and not in your own. And you will violate the law if another house invites you. They will also violate the law."

Once a month I try to meet with other people. I go at night, because the police station is next door to my house. Since my arrest, the police have confiscated Bibles and books from my home. They saw that all of the Bibles were new. So they said, "You are the leader of the group, so you know where the Bibles and materials are from."

I said that I really didn't know, because when the Bibles arrived I had been arrested. I didn't know where they came from. Now we have some Bibles again, but many people still do not have one.

CHAPTER 12

A Great Need for Training

The Blood of Jesus

The first time I held a meeting, I led a song of praise to the Lord, then prayed and shared from the Word. Even though I was a new Christian, there were 50 people in my home for this meeting.

The police heard about it. When they arrived, they did not search our meeting place, but took me to the police station for questioning. They kept me there for three days.

They put me in a cell. It was raised up off of the ground and was made of iron with many holes and was very hot inside. There were no walls on the top half, just bars all the way across the top, like a cage in a zoo. I sat down near the bottom wall. There was an old metal door with a lock on the outside. I could not see out. They fed me rice and salt in a small bowl.

At that time, I had been a Christian for two or three months, but I didn't know much about Jesus. I prayed to God and sang songs. I worried about the church, because the Christians were very new. Perhaps since I was in prison, they would be scared.

Quang Xuan

One day the police took me out of the cage to their office for questioning. They asked, "Would you abandon this religion?" They also asked me for names of other Christians, but I refused. They finally asked me, "Now do you still believe in Jesus? If we release you, will you continue to organize meetings? If you continue to meet, we will continue to arrest you."

I told them, "If you arrest me, I will just continue. I cannot stop the meetings."

After that, they took me home on a motorbike. When we arrived at the village, all the neighbors came out and the children ran out to hug me. Everyone was very happy. They asked me, "What happened in prison?" I encouraged them to invite people to our home for a meeting. Thirty people came.

I have been a Christian for three years now. I would begin my Christian life again, even if I knew that I would suffer what I have suffered all over again. I would still believe, even if I must suffer more.

Our village has about 150 families. We live very deep in the jungle. We have thatch roofs and use bamboo for poles and to build the walls. I was the first one to receive Jesus in my family. At that time, my wife and five children did not believe in Him. Then the Lord did a strange miracle in our home. When we sat together for a meal, we saw blood in the rice dishes. My wife was very surprised. I quietly shared the gospel with her about how Jesus shed blood on the cross so that we might know Him, and she believed in Jesus. Now we are all Christians. My family then joined in a meeting with our relatives. When they were dishing up the rice, blood appeared on their plates.

My wife called the neighbors to come and see what was happening. Many neighbors were curious about this, so they came to my house and joined the meeting, worshipping the Lord. Many were healed and learned about the blood of Jesus.

Bomb-hole Baptisms
Pastor Hai and another leader dug around a pond that was made when a bomb exploded. The bomb hole was as big as a

room. The Christians dug it deeper to make a pool; the water was about one-meter deep.

All the members ready to be baptized were gathered together in a house. After Pastor Hai preached to us, we walked to the pool just 50 meters in Binh Long, a S'tieng tribal area. We stood around the hole singing, "I have decided to follow Jesus, no turning back." Eleven were baptized in the pool that day, including me. Most were young people. About 30 to 40 people attended the service, including many brothers and sisters from other districts.

In the Face of Opposition

There are three villages with house churches in this area. About 18 believers had a Bible in our village. Sometimes we make the long trip to Ho Chi Minh City to look for Bibles. New Christians don't have Bibles because there are usually not enough; only the workers have a Bible. After new believers are trained by workers, they can receive a Bible if one is available.

The bomb hole was as big as a room. The Christians dug it deeper to make a pool.

The second time I was arrested, the police put me in prison for 11 days. The police asked me, "Who gives you permission to do this?"

I answered, "There is no person who has given me permission, only God."

They responded, "Even the pastors are afraid to go and share the gospel. Then how can you preach the gospel? You are just a normal Christian."

I replied, "If the Bible says that only the pastor can preach the gospel, then I would not preach. But the Bible does not say that. All Christians are to go and preach the gospel. Because of that, I go."

Then they threatened, "If you continue to preach, we will arrest you and put you in prison for 20 years."

I said, "Praise the Lord. If God permits me to live in prison for 20 years, I will accept this with joy."

The police continued to take me to the office and question me. All the police were drunk and tried to force me to smoke, but I refused. They said, "If you do not smoke, we will beat you."

I said, "If the law taught you that you must force me to smoke, and I refused and you beat me, it is your right. But the law does not teach that. If you force me and also beat me until death, I still will not smoke."

After that, they sent me back to the cell. There were ten people in this cell. I shared the gospel with the prisoners. I told them that God loved the world.

They asked, "How does God love the world?" They didn't know.

I said, "God came to this world as Jesus, and He died on the cross for us. He redeemed our sinful lives from eternal death." They listened to the gospel with interest but they did not accept Jesus.

The next morning, before the police released me, they threatened again, "If we let you go home, will you continue to organize meetings? If you continue to meet together, we will continue to arrest you."

I said, "If you want to arrest me, you do it. I cannot stop the meetings."

So the police went to my village and gathered all the people in the village and accused me before them. They have done this before on seven different occasions, yet I continue to organize meetings, and the police still come. When Christians see the police, they pray with me and cry out to the Lord.

One day, the village committee received a notice to send me to the district police station. They did not read me any rights or write a report; they just put me in prison at the Loc Ninh district police station. If the authorities want to punish anyone, they tell the prisoners inside to beat him. And if the beaten man reports to the higher authority, then they will say it was the prisoners who did the beating. This happened to me.

These prisoners were working for the police. Three people beat me at the same time. At first I just knelt down and prayed to the Lord. They pulled me up and continued to hit me. They had me face a wall and kicked me until I fell down and passed out. I was out for about an hour.

The floor was cement. There was blood in my mouth, nose, and ears. My face was swollen and there was a sore in the back of my head. The prisoners just said, "Come here," and tried to force me to eat.

I said, "I cannot eat at this time."

They said, "Do you want us to beat you again?"

I said, "No, but I must pray with the Lord before I eat the food."

They let me pray, but I could not eat because my face was swollen.

The police had put me in prison for nine days. After they released me, I drove my motorbike back home. All the children cried because they saw me like this. I wanted to comfort them, but I could not talk well. I told them that I was beaten by the prisoners.

I was in bed for 20 days. My whole body was in pain and my eyes would not open. My wife stayed at home with the children, so she took care of me while I recovered.

Christians in my village brought me to the Binh Long area, where there are many Christians who pray for the sick. The elders in the church prayed for me for many days. I became able to walk and go to the hospital. I came back and the church continued to pray, and my body became well as God healed me.

Gospel to the Khmer

After a few months, I went to a place in Kampuchea (Cambodia). In the Khmer tribe, many people—Christians and non-Christians—join together in pole houses. There were 200 people who came to know the Lord over the last few months. The greatest need is for training. Brothers and sisters know that if they receive the Word and accept Jesus, they will be persecuted. They accept the Word of the Lord and are united.

After I preached the gospel in this new place, many people received Jesus. Non-Christians came and brought guns to scare them. The non-Christians said that if the Christians continued to believe in Jesus and meet together, they would shoot them.

There was a captain in the Cambodian army who had received Jesus. I wanted him to come to our community to preach the gospel. I went to invite him, but he had left already.

Another nearby community heard about what was happening and invited me to talk about Jesus. About 70 people accepted Christ in this village. The people live back in the jungle near the Cambodian border.

My skin is the same color as the Khmer and I can speak the language. One time there were two people, one of them a lady, traveling with me. We must dress like

Cambodian people. The Cambodians usually wear a sarong. The woman, a worker in my church, dressed like my wife. There is a road in the jungle, but the way to Cambodia is very difficult. We usually arrive at midnight by walking all day and half the night.

I try to carry little Bible tracts with me and one Bible. I would rather carry the literature than food, so I don't bring food with me. Sometimes we run into wild animals. We can hear the voice and see the footprints of the tigers. There are many snakes.

We are in the midst of two or three wars. The people follow jungle law and jungle authority, which is like witchcraft and animism. They worship the plants and rocks. When we are walking on the trail, we pray constantly. We are not scared of the jungle, but we are scared of the Vietnamese border police. If we meet them along the way, they will shoot us because they think we have a relationship with the Khmer Rouge.

Sometimes we meet soldiers who want to shoot me, but I say, "In the name of Jesus, I bind up this thing." They put down their guns and let me go.

The Khmer believe in Jesus, but no one goes to teach them or preach. I share with them about our walk with Jesus, about John the Baptist, and the meaning of water baptism. After preaching to them about the meaning of water baptism, I bring them to the Mung River. We walk down the side of the river. When I am baptizing these people, they sing songs.

The local government wants to arrest us, but I usually leave before they come.

Matthew 28:18–20 are my favorite verses:

> Jesus came and spoke to them, saying, "All authority has been given to Me in heaven and on earth. Go therefore and make disciples of all the nations, baptizing them in the name of the Father and of the Son and of the Holy Spirit, teaching them to observe all things that I have commanded you; and lo, I am with you always, even to the end of the age."

CHAPTER 13

Under Constant Threat

Walking with Christ

Before the Communists came, 80 percent of the people had given their lives to Christ in Dong Cai Province. After the Communists took over my country in 1975, they called all the believers together to curse and mock them. They said to the believers, "Now you have to sign a paper to denounce your faith." They began to put a lot of pressure on these people.

Fourteen years after the Communist takeover, only four families living there were following Christ. The people in our village were not allowed to pray together at night. The Communists still watch them.

My wife and I live in a house with two rooms. We have two children, one pig, and a water buffalo. One night when my wife and I were sleeping, a voice woke me up telling me to open my Bible to Luke 10:27. I woke my wife and took the Bible from under my pillow. When I read the Scripture, it came alive for me, and my

Dinh Tan Vinh

wife and I began to pray about "loving my neighbor."

After I became a Christian, a preacher named Hao Anh came to visit me. He asked if there were any believers left in our province. I knew that his visit was the will of God. My family was encouraged and desired to go into ministry.

We began reaching out to others and helped to revive that village for the Lord. At the beginning of 1995, almost a hundred people gave their lives to Christ. There are only three families left who have not made a decision yet.

I usually go from Dong Cai to another village on my bicycle. When my bike needs repairs, I borrow another one. Sometimes I ride up to 30 kilometers. My ministry is with the K'ho tribe of nearly 200,000 people. On most of my trips, I have no literature to take, as we have very few Bibles.

I love to minister to others, because the Lord has done some wonderful things in my life. In 1989, there was a person who was offended with me. In our tribal culture, whenever someone hates another person, they offer a sacrifice to the spirit world. This person made a small coffin, as if for a little boy, and tried to call my spirit into it. He then buried the coffin and covered it with water. Sometime later, a man digging under the ground looking for gold found this coffin with an image of me.

Someone had told me that if somebody sacrificed your life, you will die. Many people acknowledged that God protected me, and because of that, many came to Christ.

This year my brother died. The people of my village prayed, and he rose from the dead! Again, many came to Christ after this happened.

There are three homes in my village where we worship. We do not have a church building. We have a Sunday service, especially when we are experiencing times of persecution. Usually I send word out about what time we will be meeting. Sometimes we meet at six o' clock in the morning. At times we are watched, so we have to meet around three o' clock in the morning. If the believers live far away, they have to get up very early to walk from their home to worship the Lord. A little less than a hundred come to my house.

When we cannot fit everyone into the room, we attach a cloth tent to the side of my house. From young to old, the people fill my house.

We use three kerosene lamps to read, but those sitting farther away cannot see to read. We sing hymns that we know by heart. The police can hear us worshipping and singing; we cannot avoid this. After worship, we go home in the dark.

Many people have accepted Christ. The police do not allow this. They call different families to the police station or court-house and ask, "Who is the preacher? Who is the evangelist?"

Christians answer, "We accept Christ, because we want to escape the bondage." The first two or three times the police call them, they are a little afraid. But after so many times, they no longer fear.

Many times the police would call me up to their station to force me to sign a paper denouncing my faith, but I refused to do it. They also came to my house. They continue to call me at the beginning of each year, even last month.

My wife and I both understand our calling, so we each serve the Lord wholeheartedly. Sometimes I go away for months to evangelize, sometimes for just two or three days. The tribal people live either in the jungle or in the mountains. They are separate from the Vietnamese people. There are twelve communities in my tribe; nine of the twelve know Christ. The other three have not had anyone receive Him.

I am a rice farmer. I harvest 184 sacks of rice, which is a miraculous amount on my small plot of land. If my field needs to be plowed with the water buffalo, I plow for a week, then go evangelize another week. My wife and some of my family—my brother, sister, or father—also help so that I can evangelize.

One day the police called me and asked, "Who gave you a license to preach? Who allows you to do this—to evangelize?"

I answered, "This is God's calling."

Then they asked me, "What do you get out of this?"

I told them, "I receive many blessings. Do you know my culture well enough? When tribal people accept Christ, we no longer have to offer sacrifices to idols."

And the Children Shall Lead Them...

My greatest desire is that the work of the Lord is expanded. I need Bibles and hymn books. I receive a few Bibles but still need more. There are 900 believers in the nearby area, but I have only six Bibles that are in Vietnamese. They have no other Christian literature, so we pass the Bibles around as I visit.

Each family gets the Bible for two days, then they pass it to another family. Then *they* pass it on. They are very happy and have peace when it's their turn to have the Bible. The younger people read Vietnamese, so the tribal families have their children read the Bible to them. The whole family, seven to nine people, will sit around the child on a straw mat on the floor.

One time I saw a 20-year-old reading to his elders.

The elders ask the younger ones, "Is this a Bible?"

The young people reply, "Yes, it is." The youth then describe a Bible character in the Bible. They read it to their father, grandfather, or mother. Every time the youth read some simple verses, all the adults understand, then they all pray and are filled with joy.

A Christmas Visit from the Police

The authorities threaten me and others in the village that if we come together and believe in Christ, they will take our things and burn our houses. So the children hide our Bible very carefully.

Last Christmas, I told everyone to come to my house for a time of worship. There are no official churches in the area, and there are 300 people in my village. We were going to celebrate the birth of Jesus.

On December 23 and 24, the Son La district police searched our house for any meat or cake, but they did not see any. They said they would stop us from celebrating if they found any.

I told them that for over 20 years we had not celebrated Christmas. The police then told me to go to the official church, but we have none in our village.

I said, "I am not going anywhere. I want to celebrate Christmas at home."

The police who came to my home on Christmas were from the tribal authorities and the Vietnamese police. They were in uniform, wearing their hats, standing in the doorway. More arrived in a Russian jeep wearing their pistols.

The police found us eating together. Over a hundred people were there; some came from far away. We had cake, candies, meat, noodles, and fish. We had taken small offerings to buy food; others brought food to put in a big bowl. We placed the food on a six-meter-long board on the straw mat floor and gathered around it. My house is so small that the believers took turns eating. Some would eat and leave.

Police ask me to step outside the door. Surprised, the police asked, "Why are you cele-brating today?"

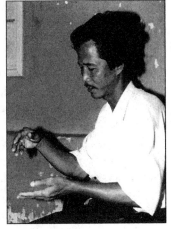

I responded, "We are Chris-tians and we gathered things to-gether to celebrate."

They said, "You surely know how to organize things. What is the purpose of this religion?"

I said, "It saves the soul."

"Save souls?"

"Yes, that is what happens. You don't have to sacrifice any-thing to idols."

I invited the officers inside. They said, "No, we do not want to eat, but do you have whiskey or wine?"

Since we had none, they left to go to a place where they could get a drink. Then they came back drunk. They brought secretaries to take notes. They tried to scold me and make things difficult.

They asked me, "Why are you doing this? Why are you together here?"

I replied, "The believers know today is Christmas, so they came. I did not gather them."

So the authorities said, "We said you cannot gather and worship God, so you can now tell them to leave."

I replied, "I am not going to chase them out. They have done nothing wrong." I went into the house. Our celebration continued, and we bowed our heads to pray.

Some of the believers asked the police, "Why don't you allow us to celebrate Christmas?"

The police began to walk back and forth, in the house and outside, wanting to control us and make things difficult for us. Again they told the believers to leave.

The believers said, "No, we are not going to leave."

I asked the police why they were trying to keep us from celebrating. I said, "Coming to God is not like coming to man. God is the Spirit, and we worship Him in spirit and in truth. Why don't you allow us to worship the Lord?"

Finally, I persuaded them to stay and observe the things that the Lord was doing in our group. I said, "If you allow us to have our faith, then we trust you more. If you do not allow us to have our faith, we will not trust you." They just laughed and shook their heads. They stayed until the believers left in the evening.

None of our new believers have been baptized. They have known the Lord for less than two years. Lord willing, I would like to baptize them someday.

I like the verse in 1 Timothy 2:4: "[God] desires all men to be saved and to come to the knowledge of the truth."

CHAPTER 14

Bibles in
Short Supply

Communism or Christ?

I had a good upbringing. I was raised in a Christian family, went to church, sang in the choir, and gave money to the ministry. I would travel, talking about Jesus to many Christians until 1975 when the Communists took over. Then I went to work for the Communist government as a teacher in the elementary school.

From 1975 to 1978, I still loved the Lord in my heart. The leader of the school asked me to attend meetings of the Communist Youth League. They asked me to become a member of the Communist Party, but not to mention Jesus. In my heart I made a decision not to do this; but from that time on, my Christian life went downhill. I didn't pray. I didn't read the Bible. My life became like other people in the world. I did everything and was not scared of anything.

In 1983, I coughed up blood. My kidneys also malfunctioned. One part of my heart could not work normally. My lungs and throat were also swollen.

Nguyen Van Dong with his son, Huang Sa

I went to the hospital for six months, but the hospital could not help me. The hospital said that my kidneys made me very weak. I was very sad and wanted to commit suicide.

One Sunday, the son of a pastor came to visit me. He asked me about my sickness. "Do you have enough money to go to the hospital?"

I shook my head and said, "No, I will die."

This brother said, "If the hospital cannot help you, there is one Person who can. He is Jesus. If you believe in Jesus, your sins will be forgiven, and your body can be healed."

At that time, I didn't believe. I wondered if God could heal me. I told this brother, "If Jesus is alive and if He heals my life, I will believe in Him and surrender my life to Him."

Soon my body began to grow stronger and I felt healthy. I began to trust in God. I went to church and told my brother and sister about the miracle God did in my life. From then on, I returned to the Lord. I used to work with the Christian Missionary Alliance (CMA) church, and many people believed in Jesus. But I desired to serve the Lord in a larger area. When I serve God, at times I get tired. I don't have enough time to study the Bible or have many opportunities to be trained.

I started to serve the Lord in children's ministry. In the central highlands we no longer have a church building. The government had closed it, so we were meeting in the house of a pastor of the Tin Lanh church. I taught Sunday school and became a deacon in this church.

In the big cities, a Christian can be a teacher. But in the central highlands, the local governments are quite strict and the persecution is very intense in some areas. Sometimes a Christian cannot become a teacher. Pleiku is one of the strictest places.

Judgment Wears Gloves

One day the government called me to the office of the vice-president of the Education Board. There were two government education officers sitting at the table wearing gloves. When they interviewed me, they wrote in a book all I had said. They questioned me for about two hours, asking me when I believed in Jesus and what I did in the church. I told them why I believe in Jesus and why I serve Him.

After that, they commanded me to write a report of what happened in my life, when I believed in Jesus, when I started to serve the Lord, and why I believe in Jesus. They left and gave me time to write.

Later when they returned to the room, they said, "Because of the decision of the high authorities, we will not allow you to continue to teach in the school."

The education officers also summoned two Christian brothers of the Banah tribe who were teachers. The Banah Christians also agreed that they would accept dismissal and leave their teaching rather than deny Christ.

My brother is also a Christian. He said, "If they will not let you teach school, you can come back and work on the farm because it is God's will." So when they dismissed me, I walked ten kilometers back to the farm and went to work.

I planted vegetables and potatoes. But in spite of the work, I took time to serve the Lord. Many times I am very tired, but that does not bother me. When I serve the Lord, I see His hand on my life and His protection even in dangerous situations.

Since 1975, the persecution in my area of Pleiku has been constant. All the churches were closed and all the pastors were kicked out of this area. They still do not allow pastors to live there, except for one Vietnamese.

According to Vietnamese propaganda, the police do not say anything about the Bible. But among the tribal people, whenever they see the Bible, they take it.

They have taken the Bibles in our area, but some Christians hid them in their houses. When we go to a house church meeting, we do not take our Bibles with us, because the police will take them. Bibles are in short supply so we go to the lowlands to ask the other Christians for a Bible. Then we hide ours in a sack.

Some Sundays we go to a meeting in Ho Chi Minh City. Since 1985, the police come and seize the Bibles, depending on the situation and their mood. They use the Bibles as evidence. One policeman with six others told us he was a captain. He stopped the meeting, wrote a report, and took all our Bibles.

Another time, 20 of us were worshipping together when the police came. They said that our Bibles were printed before 1975 (Communist rule), so they were not allowed. They took all the Bibles, hymn books, and other materials—about 38 kilograms (80 pounds) of books—from the pastor's house and never returned them. Some of the brothers at the meeting did not bring their Bibles.

The American Emperor

In the Tin Lanh church, some officials say that Christianity is a religion that comes from the Europeans and Americans, since many missionaries came from America and Europe to evangelize Vietnam. They brought the Word, which the police say is like an "American emperor coming to Vietnam." [*Editor's note:* Since the 1600s, Vietnamese rulers have consistently opposed Christianity.]

Some brothers and sisters bring Bibles for us and for the Christians in the lowlands, and we carry these to the highlands. But the tribal people still lack Bibles, and do not have much freedom to worship.

I went to evangelize the Banah and Jo'Rai tribes. Whenever I go

The young teach the old about Jesus with illustrated story books smuggled into the country.

there, I always encounter persecution from the government. Spies usually follow us. Some villages are 90 percent Christian, so people do not report us. But in some villages with about 50 percent Christians, the other non-Christians will instantly report to the police if they see any strange person, like a foreigner or Vietnamese.

On our way home, the police usually stop us on the road and arrest us. If we are with the local pastors, the police say we work together with the Americans and the Europeans to invade the country. They say the local pastor is a spy for the foreigners. The police have followed me many times and have commanded all of the people in the village, "If you see Nguyen Dong in this village, report it to us immediately."

In certain places I must travel at night, sometimes by bicycle, sometimes on foot. The farthest village, about 50 kilometers away, may take four hours travel time; other places take two hours. I carry only one Bible, which I put on the back of my bicycle or hide it on my body. I use a flashlight, holding it with one hand and guiding the bicycle with the other. Sometimes my light jerks all around the road because the roads are not flat. Usually the road has many rocks, and a lot of gravel and dirt. There are many "elephant" holes (big holes). Sometimes I fall off my bike and get scratched, especially in the rainy season.

I have to go through streams, and in some places the water is very deep. There may be a bridge, usually a tree with a wooden handrail. I must put my Bible in a plastic bag, then tie it on the back of my bicycle so it never gets wet.

I do not take any food with me. They usually feed me in the village. The food of the tribal people is different from Vietnamese food. They serve rice, fish, chicken, squirrels, rabbit, and sometimes jungle pig. To catch these wild animals, they use traps made with a bent tree limb and a circle of rope. If an animal approaches, the rope will catch them and hang them in the air. If the people don't have meat, they eat rice with salt.

I helped start some house churches in these tribes. A tribal Christian goes with me to visit his relatives in another village where we develop relationships, then we share about Jesus. Although people know Vietnamese, I must use the Banah language to talk with them. They do not accept Jesus immediately. We must visit with them many times before they do.

Once my bicycle broke down on the way to a village. Because I stopped to repair it, I was late. I arrived 15 minutes after the police left the village. The Lord's hand was in that! My bicycle never broke down again.

On May 28, 1993, in the Mang Giang district, all the Christians in a village joined together. As new people came to our prayer meeting, we continued in prayer for the village for days. On May 30, there were 61 new converts. The news traveled throughout the village. I heard then that the police were coming. I asked God what I should do. I felt the Lord saying that since I had His love, I would not be scared. I sensed the Lord wanted me to stay there.

I stayed at the meeting until two policemen came. The police arrested me that morning, and took me in handcuffs to the district police station. There they took my picture and fingerprints. My solitary cell was three meters by two and a half meters. There was a cement slab for a bed, and a hole in the floor for a toilet. The only light came from a small window.

The "Cattle" Drive

That afternoon, 40 Banah Christians joined together in the same meeting when 30 police came in a jeep, on foot, and on motorbikes to arrest them.

These 40 Christians walked quietly to the police station, herded between the motorcycles and jeep. Each day for three days, the Christians walked one kilometer back and forth from their village so the police could interrogate them at the station. I climbed up the wall holding the iron door to look outside. I saw the believers walking on the road.

At that time, I had two children and my wife was expecting another in about ten days. She came to visit me before she gave birth. I had already been in prison six days.

She got up early in the morning for the trip and rode on the bicycle 20 kilometers carrying our two girls on the back. The police gave her two hours to visit me. My wife was smiling. She brought me a mosquito net.

Our family prayed together in the prison yard. As we sat on the ground, our two daughters came over to sit in our laps. My wife asked me what I was eating and about the conditions in the prison. She was afraid that they would beat me.

I said, "This is the work of God, so I am ready to accept this. Go back to take care of the children." We said a simple goodbye and she left with the girls.

I was in that prison only ten days. Each day after interrogation, I spent time singing and praying in my cell. After they released me, my wife gave birth to a girl.

When I prayed to God, He gave me Jeremiah 33:3: "Call to Me, and I will answer you, and show you great and mighty things..." Whenever I go to preach the gospel, God gives me a verse in the Bible, such as Exodus 23:20, "Behold, I send an angel before you to keep you in the way and to bring you into the place which I have prepared."

In 1992, a brother from Ho Chi Minh City came to organize a seminar. In the area where I go to evangelize, there are about 30,000 Christians among the Banah and Jo'Rai tribes. We go there and teach them, and sometimes have Bibles to bring to them. We could only bring about 100 Banah and Jo'Rai language Bibles and about 200 Vietnamese Bibles. So they have only 300 Bibles for 30,000 Christians.

CHAPTER 15

Willing to Die

Before the "Sanhedrin"

Because I obey the Lord, the police have arrested me for preaching the gospel. After 12 days, the police brought me back to the village and put me before all the people like a people's court. They brought a video camera to tape me. The city authorities also came down to this area. As I stood before the people, they said, "No foreign religion, only one religion— the religion of Uncle Ho." [3] They said that I was the one who caused all the chaos in this area. They asked the people to sentence me to death.

The people raised up their hands, voting with their fists in the air. They wanted my throat cut. Let me tell you how this all began...

At midnight on February 23, 1987, the Lord called me. I was very touched and cried. I was born in a Christian family, but didn't know the Lord. I joined the army for three years and was sick with malaria for a year and a half. I was treated with medicine, but was not cured. Then the Lord touched me. I went to a church and listened to

To Dinh Trung

---

[3] Ho Chi Minh was the first Communist leader of Vietnam.

the message that the pastor gave about the healing of the Lord. I came home and read in the Bible about this. I cried out in my heart to the Lord and said, "You are God. You can do a miracle in my life. Change my life." All night I cried to the Lord and prayed until I felt a heavy weight fall off my soul. I felt no more sickness in my body.

The Lord gave me a hunger and passion to read the Bible. I renounced worshipping idols. I decided to organize worship meetings in my home to continue studying the Word with this new faith in the Lord. We no longer lived a life that was like the world's family, like eating the food that was offered to idols, or other sins.

I was very simple and didn't understand much, but I loved the Lord and would meet with a preacher named Doan to share the gospel. We would go out to preach to different areas.

The K'ho Tribe
Later, in 1991, I contacted some friends I knew in Tra Bong. These are the K'ho tribal people. This tribe has darker skin.

The village of the K'ho is next to a big waterfall and is very beautiful. The K'ho houses are on the ground, not up on poles, with thatch roofs and thick woven thatched walls. The rain cannot go through the thatched walls. They have dirt floors with one big room. They raise pigs on the land around their houses.

The first time I visited was very amazing. I know a K'ho tribal man whose name is Ho Hoang Duy. When this man was a nonbeliever, he went to a Catholic home and saw a Bible. The Lord caused him to want that book so much that he asked this Catholic man to give him the book. The man gave it to him and he went back home. He read it cover to cover.

I went down to Binh Son to see if there were any Christians there. But I found out that the gospel had never penetrated this area. I found Brother Doan and we became close friends. At that time, he was facing a lot of difficulties. He was very poor, so I helped him build his house. I called the other K'ho people to come help with the mud wall, dirt floor, and roof.

As we worked, we shared jobs, the Word, and the gospel. Many people came from nearby villages and received Jesus. The government was very surprised, because there used to not be any Christians here. The government searched to find out who organized and brought the gospel to these people.

The Rice Thieves

The people told them that Mr. Doan went there to share. The government tried to find ways to arrest him. First they arrested Brother Duy, who was the first Christian there. They beat him up. They took away his possessions and all of his rice from the harvest. They took away his pigs, his bicycle, and a small machine to clean the rice.

Soon the soldiers of the village came with the district police, carrying rifles. They wanted him to renounce his faith,

The police took the ox of Brother Loc, shot it, cut up the meat, and ate it.

but Brother Duy didn't react. He calmly just let them take his things. His wife and four children stood beside him.

The soldiers carried baskets on their backs and poured the rice into them. They carried the rice to the village office and later took it to the district office to eat.

This was the twenty-third time Brother Duy and other Christians were arrested. The police brought them all down to the district police station. The police said they wanted to build

Ho Van Loc is in prison

up the tribe's religious unity again to reject the "Western" Jesus and continue to worship a vague god and their ancestors. They worship the "fathers." They took the ox of Brother Loc [featured in VOM's April 1994 newsletter] and shot it with their rifles, cutting up the meat right in front of him. Then they offered the meat to their idols and tried to force all the Christians to eat this idol-worship meat, but they would not. Whoever refused to eat it was considered a bad person. The police brought wine that they offered to idols, then they ate the whole ox.

Brother Loc's wife and children were very sad. Their only possession was the ox that they used to plow the field. They eat many white potatoes with little nutritional value. So for years they have suffered. I often go there to help them. Their faith is very good, and they continue to trust God and meet for worship. Loc plants rice on a hill and also plants bananas. He still needs another ox.

Arrested Twenty-four Times

Then the twenty-fourth time we were arrested, the police came to get me. When I entered Tra-Bong, some people saw me and reported me to the government. That is why they arrested me.

They used a gun and told me to be still. They brought me down to the district station in Tra-Bong where they accused me and put me in prison. They incarcerated me for twelve days and did not allow me to eat.

In prison I worshipped the Lord a lot, praying and singing in a room by myself. My room was the prison toilet. It was in an isolation cell about two meters square. It was very dark and dirty with no windows. They did not allow me to bring anything inside. The mosquitoes could freely bite me. Since there was no sewage drain in there, the smell was terrible. I could not bathe. I got a high fever like malaria.

The Christian brothers in Tra-Bong sent food to me. The police pushed rice and water through a small hole. When I would sing a children's song, "Love the Lord day and night," the guards would get very angry with me. They shouted and threatened me, "You are not allowed to sing loud in the prison!"

Everyday the police brought me to their work room for questioning. Usually only three policemen questioned me. They changed all the time. They had the city police, the district police, and the village police. I was able to tell many policemen about the gospel.

Preaching "Illegally"

They would hit me and ask, "Why do you come here? Who sent you to the Tra-Bong area?"

I told them that I went by myself. "The Lord told me to share the gospel with them."

They asked, "Who gave you the documents to preach the gospel? Did you receive the pastor's certificate?"

I replied, "I am not a pastor. I am a Christian, and I obey the Lord to go out and share the Word with others.

They asked, "Where do you go to church?"

I told them I went to an official church in Binh Son on Sundays.

After 12 days, the police brought me back to the village before all the people where the police wanted to cut my throat.

I became bold and grabbed the microphone. Speaking to the people, I said, "For the Lord's sake, because of His name, I am willing to die."

The police grabbed the microphone back, exclaiming, "Once again, you want to preach the gospel."

Then the Communists brought the people's court down to the Binh Son district. They held me there for ten more days in the jail. The Communists, city police, district police, and village police would not cut my throat, but they would fine me one buffalo and 1,000,000 Vietnamese dong. They said the "people" asked for a fine of one buffalo, so they could sacrifice it to idols and reinforce religious traditions in the area. I had to find 1,000,000 Vietnamese dong for a penalty.

I came from another district, so they sent me back to my own district police because I had no money. I went on a bus with one policeman, and they brought me out before the people's court again in the Binh Hai village. My wife was also at the people's court. She did not cry, but was very happy. She was standing on the people's side.

These police treated me the same way, despising me and humiliating me. They said, "You are preaching illegally."

The police tried their best to name many crimes I committed, but the people did not believe them. They knew that I was a good person, preaching the gospel. The police released me.

Many official churches are very afraid of contact with the police. The Binh Son church is an official church of 30 members. When the Binh Son church knew that I had been arrested, they refused to let me worship with them. They scolded me and said I brought

To Dinh Trung's family waits for his release

problems and chaos. They isolated me, not allowing me to come to church. They told me that I made the police come to their church at Binh Son and interfere with them, and they didn't like it. Since they no longer have fellowship with me, I just stay by myself and pray alone.

After praying for a while, the Lord led Brother Loc and another brother to visit me at midnight one time. Brother Loc encouraged me to go on a mission trip. At first, I didn't trust him. But after we studied and shared in the Word, I was convinced and decided to go out and preach the gospel again.

I joined another brother in the mission field in the Quang Ninh area.

The police arrested me once again. They asked, "Who do you go to church with? Who do you fellowship with? Do you have a church? Do you have the government's permission?"

I said, "We have the permission of God."

They asked where we meet. We replied, "We meet at home." Then they began watching my home.

My favorite Bible verse is, "The Lord is my Shepherd" (Psalm 23:1). That verse gave me strength in prison.

My wife was very happy when the Lord allowed my imprisonment and these other things to happen. I have a wife and two children, and a baby coming soon. My oldest child is six years old and the other is three. My wife always supports me in my ministry. Some of my friends from the official church say that the Lord is with me and encourage me.

[*Editor's note:* At press time of this book, To Dinh Trung, the witness in this chapter, and Ho Van Loc are serving a three-year prison sentence for evangelism. Please write an encouraging letter to them. Their prison address is: Trai Giam Tinh, Quâng Ngãi, Vietnam.]

CHAPTER 16

The Healing Place

His Healing Hand

In 1986 I got an infection on my face, but because of the love of God I did not die. It was just like in Psalm 118:18, "The Lord has chastened me severely, but He has not given me over to death."

The sickness lasted for six months. During the first three months, I could still work in the fields, but I had a headache and a runny nose. In the fourth month, the doctor gave me medicine to drink and said that I would need an operation. In the fifth month, I could no longer work.

The growth broke out terribly and spread into my eyes and ears. There was no more pain, but my whole face was just numb. I could only drink grape juice or orange juice. I could not breathe through my nose. My teeth had to be pulled one right after the other because they were rotten. I constantly fought off flies. The doctor said it would take many operations and that the infection would destroy my bones. He told me to go to the Saigon Hospital to have one eye removed; the surgeons would open up my face and try to cure it.

Chung Truong

However, in Phan Rang, there are three pastors. One pastor agreed to move me, but the others said there was no need to. Since my family did not have any money, the pastors hesitated and finally decided not to take me to Saigon. Sadly, they all left me at home to wait for my death.

Finally, the doctors told me there was no more hope. They said 90 percent of these cases die, so there was no need to go to Saigon for treatment. They said if I fell with this swollen face, it would be crushed like a watermelon. The doctor had told me that by the end of March, I would go crazy and die. I praise the Lord that we had no money. If we had, they would have taken me to Saigon and the doctors would have taken out an eye.

Instead, the Lord used a Christian from Saigon who had been cured of an infection. She returned to Phan Rang to give a testimony. We invited this Christian into our home church to give her testimony. They brought me to the meeting in a chair. I smelled so terrible that people tried to sit far away from me. The pastor's wife and the lady who gave her testimony lovingly sat beside me. The Lord used the words in Isaiah 53 and Psalm 103. My family grabbed onto that promise of the Lord, believing that He would save me.

When she said, "By His stripes we are healed," I felt some power lift my head up and a beam of light come down on me. I rose up.

The pastor's wife and the other Christians thought that now I had gone crazy. I fell down unconscious, so the family took me home.

The following week, I just lay there. I could drink no more juice and take no more medicine on my face. But the infection began to fall away. I became conscious again and I started to repent of all my sins in detail. God began to heal me and forgave all my wickedness.

One day, the family and Christians in the Phan Rang church fasted and prayed for me from six o'clock in the morning until five o'clock in the evening. They brought me back to an official Tin Lanh church. Although the Lord had begun to heal me, it looked like this was to be the last day of my life. My husband said, "If the Lord does not heal her, there is no more hope."

The people continued to physically lift me up each time I lay down—five times in that afternoon. At five o'clock I started to look up a little bit. I saw a cross with a light coming straight upon me. I felt very hot under my feet. The heat moved up in my body, and the higher it moved, the more I could kneel with my back straight. Finally, the beam went straight to my face, and I heard something like boiling inside my face. I hiccupped and said, "Hallelujah." According to Psalm 103:1–4, God delivered me and healed my sickness:

> Bless the Lord, O my soul; and all that is within me, bless His holy name!
> Bless the Lord, O my soul, and forget not all His benefits:
> Who forgives all your iniquities, who heals all your diseases,
> Who redeems your life from destruction, who crowns you with lovingkindness and tender mercies.

My face was completely clean. I could breathe through my nose again. I could kneel straight; no one needed to hold me. I stood up, ran and jumped all around the church. The infection had fallen on the floor. My face was full of light.

The pastor in that church, Pastor Tam, preached about the power of God; but he had never actually seen God's power. The pastor said, "Mrs. Truong, you didn't wash your face yet." When he saw the Lord heal me, he also prayed and experienced the Lord's healing of a constant headache. He began to pray for many other sicknesses. Many people who were sick also received healing from God.

In this big city, there are only three churches, and two had been closed by the government. Two hundred thousand people live there with only one official Protestant church open. Pastor Tam's church is just a small one. At Christmas time, they can gather 1,000 members.

Before I was healed, I never stood before the church and spoke. I only followed my husband and became a Christian. I didn't understand or change; but in the morning I stood before Pastor Tam's church and gave my testimony.

In this area of Vietnam, there is one tribe: the Cham people. The city of Phan Rang had three churches, but the authorities had closed down two. The only remaining church is Pastor Hieu's. In the afternoon, I went to Pastor Hieu's church and gave my testimony. Many people came and received healing, and many visitors accepted Christ.

A Healing Message to a Hurting People

I continued to go to five churches—in Saigon and Da Lat—to share my testimony. Pastor Tu asked me to pray for another woman who was diagnosed with five sicknesses. She was also healed and is now serving the Lord.

The day I came back, Pastor Tam had been arrested and held for 20 days. The authorities confiscated the church building. My home church at Tapcham is in a suburb five kilometers away. The police had also closed my church, and they arrested me. The police thought that sharing my testimony was a plot of the Americans. Since I was very poor, they thought I would tell lies about the power of God like this to cause trouble. So they put me in prison. Because this was the first time I was arrested, I did not know what an arrest was.

The doctor said that if I was isolated in this place with dirty air and not enough meat and fish, my sickness might come back again. The police would not allow my family to send any food from home in case they put some medicine in it so I could be healed. Then my family would lie and say that the Lord healed me.

A Prostitute in Stocks

The police treated me very badly for one month and five days. Because I preached the gospel, I was put in isolation. My room was one meter wide by one and a half meters long. There was no light. I stood and sat, but there was not enough room to lie down. Mostly I prayed and did not sleep. There was no chair so I had to sit on the dirty floor. I was very hungry with only a little ball of rice and salt. I prayed to the Lord and saw the Lord stand by me and strengthen me. I poured water into the rice to soften it and ate a little bit; I just swallowed it. But I also did not want to eat at times. I wanted to fast and pray.

In my cell was a small hole for air. In front of the door, there was a small square window where they would hand in the food and water. They just pushed it in and left right away. They poured a cup of water into a plastic bag inside. We had to be prepared to take it. If we were not ready, they would pour the water in on the floor, and there would no more for that day.

I could not lie down. I sat upon the board and shared the gospel with this girl.

Ten days later they brought a prostitute into my cell. The police put her there for a week to threaten me. She came from a bigger prison and was about 28 years old. This prostitute had a wooden stock between her legs. It was a board with about six big holes in it and the prostitute's feet were placed in the two widest holes, so there were four holes in between her feet. Then these two big wooden pieces were locked together. When the prostitute sat on the floor, her legs were spread with her feet in this board on this one-meter floor. She had violated the law in another cell, so they imprisoned her with the board to discipline her.

I stood in one corner to give some space to her. If the girl laid down, I sat up. I could not lie down, because the board took up the space in our small cell. When I felt tired, I sat on the board. Then I would stand up. I ended up standing all day and night.

I shared the gospel with this girl, but she was fearful. "If the guards listen outside and hear you preaching the gospel, they will separate us," she said.

I talked to her about Jesus anyway. I told her, "Look at your sad life. Look at your situation. The Lord can heal your life."

She looked up and said, "You are older than me, but you are so bold to preach and be charged with a crime that is not a crime." She received Jesus. As I prayed for her, she was crying. When she left that place, she asked God for strength to no longer be a prostitute.

The police would wake me up at one or two o'clock in the morning for more questioning. Three policemen worked with me. They asked, "Who sent you out? Who taught you how to go out and talk in different places like this? Who pays you to do this?"

Although my cell was very dirty and dark, I confessed that since the Lord healed me, the sickness would not return. I felt very strong. One morning, at one o'clock, the guards called me out to the work room where they threaten the prisoners.

They have handcuffs, pistols, rifles, and a thick hose. They have the eight-hole stock and different things in this room.

There were about seven policemen; they sat at a table while I stood. Generally, the guards were North Vietnamese. The policeman who interrogated me every day is an officer in charge of religious matters from the province that sent him there. I remember the names of two other men—Mr. Ky and Mr. Thanh—who are policemen from Thuan Hai Province.

Only the prison policemen wore uniforms. The city policemen wore civilian clothes when they worked with me, so I didn't know what rank they were. I preached the gospel a lot to them. They had many papers they had to stamp while they questioned me.

The police gave me a big sheet of paper with typing on it and blanks to fill in information. They told me that if I said I was still sick, they would release me right away; but if I said I was well, they would sentence me to three years in prison.

I said to them, "I know for sure the Lord has healed me already."

So they said, pointing at the stocks, "If you say you are no longer sick, you will be put in there, six holes between your feet for one month."

I replied to the police, "I will not sign that because I am not sick. God healed me. If I am still sick, I agree to be put in the stocks with *eight* holes—not six!"

A Doctor's Conscience

They tried another method. After a month and five days, the police took me to the hospital to reexamine me. The night before they took me to the doctor, they gave me the paper to sign. "If the doctor finds you well, you will be released; but if you are still sick, you will go into one of the three prisons— Song Mao, Song Cai, or Song Luy." They thought that I had lied, that I was still sick. They wanted me to deny that God had healed me. The police continued to threaten me, and to pressure me to confess that I was sick before they brought me to the examination.

I signed the assurance that if the doctor says, "You are sick," I was willing to go to one of these prisons. I knew for sure that the Lord had healed me and there was no more sickness.

That morning they took me to the doctor in a covered truck. The police all sat in front, and I was in a cage in the very back. There was a cover on the outside so the public would not see anyone.

When we arrived at the hospital, the two soldiers in uniform pushed me into the doctor's examination room right away. The police took me to the same doctor who had treated me before. This doctor was in charge of checking the prisoners. He was Catholic, but he was also under the pressure of the police.

When the doctor realized who I was, he was surprised, thinking I had died three months ago. I shared with him a saying we use in Vietnam, "A good doctor is like a good mother. When you check me, tell the truth about me, then my God will bless you. If you do not tell the truth about me, then you will have to receive the results God will give you."

One of the policemen slapped his hand on the table and shouted, "Quiet! No more talking!" Then he pushed me down in a chair.

I had not eaten for two days or slept for two nights. I was not thinking about my family, only about communing with God. I said to the Lord, "Strengthen me so I can be strong. Lord, I am very hungry, so strengthen me, so I can breathe strongly." The Lord gave me a special strength. I can still remember it just like it was yesterday.

The policeman closely watched the doctor as he examined my nose, eyes, ears, and mouth. He asked me to breathe. He was looking with a small flashlight, but saw no evidence of my infection. I was completely healed.

The doctor said, "Truly, your God saved you." The police heard it.

I replied, "Yes, my God saved me. He healed me already."

The doctor turned to the policeman and changed the words a little bit, using the pagan term for God, so the policeman would understand. He did this by calling God "Troi" (meaning god), just like the highest being. The doctor said to the police, "The highest being has saved her."

The two policemen pushed me outside, then spoke with the doctor at his desk. Through the window on the door to the examination room, I saw them talking. They asked him to give them a paper that confessed I was still sick. He continued to shake his head "no." Finally, the doctor stood up, and the police were very angry. They just grabbed the paper and walked out. The doctor also walked out. As he passed me, he said, "My conscience would not allow me."

When the police brought me back to prison, they did not keep their promise to release me if I was well. They could not accept the fact that the Lord really healed me. They called me from my cell and held the doctor's paper up far away from me. "See, the doctor said you are still sick. You work for the Americans. You are not healed."

Then I responded, "Hold that paper up to me, closer."

They wouldn't give it to me. Later they took me to a bigger prison.

Forty prisoners were inside my cell. I felt more at ease because of the bigger space. The women went out to work during the day and came back at night. To sleep, many of us would have to lie on our side on the floor to have enough space. The women asked what serious political crime I had committed to be put in here. I told them I had only preached the gospel.

In Vietnam when we get sick, we often rub some oil on our skin, then use a spoon to move the skin to clear out the pores. I did this to help many of the prisoners feel better. When the policemen got sick, I helped them too.

The people in the isolated cells were also sick. When they tried to bring these people to the hospital, they were afraid and often tried to hide or to rebel. Many times they brought these sick people to my room to help them, so my cell became a healing place. I prayed for them and shared the gospel with them. Many received Jesus in my cell.

The authorities called me "the 180-degree troublemaker," which is the "worst" kind. The police continued to question me, "Who sent you? What organization sent you?"

I would reply each time, "The Lord Jesus. If you dare, you arrest the Lord Jesus."

They wanted to transfer me to the other prisons that they had mentioned before. The prisoners I was with at that time had committed different social crimes—murdering, stealing, prostitution—and were waiting to be transferred to other prisons. They sent the prostitutes to Song Mao. Robbers and murderers were sent to Song Luy, and others were sent to Song Cai. The police finally decided to send me to Song Mao. But first they took my fingerprints and my picture. My prison number was 1013.

I waited for transfer. In my cell many new Christians were also waiting. I tried to encourage them. I took out a hairpin and scratched a cross on the wall. This was the first Sunday of the month. Usually in church we have Communion. We didn't have bread, only a little bit of water. As we knelt on the floor, I shared with these prisoners, now my sisters, about Communion and drank water with them.

On the Third Day...Released

I stayed up all that night to pray to the Lord. I said, "May Your will be done. If You want me to go out tomorrow, release me from this camp. Do a miracle. If You want me to be in prison for three more years, I think I will be weak and not have enough of the Word to be strengthened after this time. But if You release me tonight, I will give my whole life to preach the gospel—everything." I asked the Lord to give me a sign that in three more days an officer would come to work with me, and that two days after that I would be released. The Lord gave me the sign exactly like that.

Signing the Papers

After three days, the people from Vien Kiem Xoat (the institute that handles court matters) came from the city and looked up my case. This was a strange thing, since this institute never looks up a case again once it is finished. I would just go to another prison. This officer carried a numbered file under his arm. He went straight to the chief guard, a policeman I had treated for illness and with whom I had shared the gospel.

The two of them came into our transfer cell. When they opened the door, everybody stood up straight. The officer called my name, "Lady Truong, come out. You are the one who created trouble by doing superstitious things, right?"

Then the chief of the prison answered for me and said, "No, she is the one who is making people push away the (pagan) altars and practices. She is a Christian."

Then the officer asked, "What is your crime?"

I said, "I have no crime."

The officer responded, "Tell me, what did you do?"

"I am a sinner. I was sick, but the Lord healed me. He used His blood to cleanse all of my sickness and all of my sin. Because of that, I share about my healing, about how the Lord saved and healed me. So that is why I believe in Jesus."

He told me to go back and sit down. They locked the door again. Exactly two days later (according to the sign that I asked from the Lord), the chief of the police station called me. This time he was very polite. He asked me to sit down, using a term like "Auntie" because of my age. He said, "Yes, truly your God healed you, but now if you will assure me that you will no longer speak about this God who heals, then, Auntie, I will let you go."

I replied, "No, I will not. If the Lord tells me to go, I will go. If He tells me to sit, I will sit."

The police in the room then asked me to write a guarantee that I would not preach the gospel. I told them that I would not sign. Finally they sent me an "order of release," which said my crime was propaganda and superstition. Seeing the paper on the desk, I pushed aside the three guards and took the pen off the desk. I just crossed over it and wrote, "The power of God, healing."

The officer laughed and said, "Now you are going home, but you still fight."

But I did not leave yet. I walked from one place to another in the prison to share about God's healing. There was a room for officers. I stayed there so I could speak to the policemen. I went to each one and said, "They have just given me this clear release sentence, no charges, because God healed me, as I have committed no crime. So even though you have a rank of authority, when you retire, you will throw this all away. You also must meet Jesus, in order to go to heaven. If you want to go to heaven, you must have Jesus as your Savior. Jesus is the God who heals and the Savior of the whole world. Serve Him." They listened to me because they had a special affection for me.

I went back home and shared with Catholics and Buddhists. The Buddhists sent more reports to the police that I continued preaching the gospel, so the police office in the village called me again to write a self-examination report. That night, I prayed instead of writing a self-examination. The next morning in the office, I wrote out an account of how the Lord healed me and my life.

They threatened, "We will take you to a re-education camp!"

I sat there with my raincoat and a small Bible. I was prepared to go to prison again. Then the local police took me to five policemen. One read my account and passed it to the next one to read until all five had read my testimony.

One said, "Oh, this is what you do. This is good. You tell the people to do good, but you must do it in a way that the people will not sue you or report you. You make them forsake their ancestor worship, forsake their religion, so they report you." Then they released me.

I kept up my ministry anyway. My eight children and two grandchildren also know of my witness. One time the policemen brought some sugar and tea to my house and visited with my husband. They instructed him to tell me not to go out preaching the gospel.

My husband said, "Because God has healed her, she is so joyful. If you have threatened her to stop, how can *I* stop her?"

The Cham Tribe

The Lord gave me a vision for the tribal people, so I started going to the K'ho tribe. The Lord also gave me a burden for the tribal people near my homeland—the Cham tribe. They have two branches of worship: Muslim and Hindu-Muslim. This tribe has a hatred for the Vietnamese, because the tribes are the ones who formerly owned the land. Then the Vietnamese came and conquered their land, destroying their nation. Now the Cham population is only about 20,000.

In one Cham group, they burn the dead and throw things at the body. They say if a rich person dies, there will be some kind of oil or something in the body that will keep it from rotting. They have funerals that last a month. They kill a buffalo, and the family

eats it for the entire month. They also invite monks and burn incense with rituals throughout this time. If the extended family requests two buffaloes, then the family whose member died must kill two buffaloes for the whole tribe to eat. Many times they are in great debt.

They use wood from a very sour fruit to burn the body. For one month they cut down this wood and prepare it. If the dead person had any possessions, others would have to "buy back his possessions." Everyone has to pay. Then they put his possessions on top of his wrapped up body into a frame to burn. The eldest son lights the fire with a long stick.

As the fire starts to get bigger and hotter, the families stand in a line on both sides of the body and throw cookies over it. The people on the other side take time to eat them, thinking that if they eat these cookies, the spirit cannot harm them.

If they throw money across the body, the other side will use that money as a charm to hang around their necks. They also throw bread and cake over to eat. After they eat, they dance. Then when the fire dies, the eldest son will use a big machete and chop off the head of the dead. He cuts it up and takes seven pieces of the head bone. He puts the seven pieces of the bone into seven jars, which they take to different villages. Each village will have one jar, and the monk will come, burn incense, and chant.

They take the ashes and bones and dump them into a field that has been divided for his share. They call the field "cuc," which means the "law field."

In this "law field," whoever wishes to plant crops has to sacrifice one child. Every year they will make a sacrifice. They bring a cart of rice up to this field. Then they bring a child up to this field and leave. They will hear a chopping sound. They say this is the "spirit field" so the spirit will eat up this child and the rice. I do not know what happens to the rice. If there are no more children, they will look for beggars' children. They will take the place of village children. I know they have offered a goat instead of a child.

At first I went by myself on the bus with a Bible. I walked the last part and met with a tribal man. I cautiously entered the village to share the Word. I had not been trained much in the Word yet, but I went anyway.

There was only one Christian pastor among the Cham. Since the time he became a pastor until the day he died, he was the only Christian.

One day, where three roads meet together, monks or gurus of some kind were offering dishes as worship or as a sacrifice to their gods. I saw they had puppets made of wool. They put 41 needles all over the body to harm a girl in the next village because an angry man could not have her in marriage; she loved someone else.

My youngest son ran to this puppet doll left by the road. He thought the puppet was cute with little needles. He wanted to take it home for something to play with. He picked up the puppet and brought it back to me. He was very happy and said, "Mom, it has many needles like this."

When others saw him with this they said, "You are going to die because you have taken this thing."

When I went home, I made a fire and threw the puppet of wool into the fire. Later the people told me that the girl had been sick, but when I threw the puppet into the fire, the girl was free from her sickness. I realized the freedom the Lord could bring to help these people. That is why I got very bold to go out. The people accused me of making their religion powerless, but they were also terrified of the ceremonies of the Cham tribe. Even the government is afraid of the Cham ceremonies. They would never stop them.

Upon arriving in one village with a Christian sister, we were offered a delicacy reserved for guests. They kept fish tied on strings and hung them from the ceiling. Breaking open the fish on our leaf plates, fat, white worms came squirming out of them. My Christian sister screamed! I leaned over and whispered to her, "We must eat this to show our love for these people." When the villagers were not looking, we quickly shook the fish and pushed the worms through the cracks of the bamboo floor. Our small sacrifice was not in vain as seventeen villages in this area came to Jesus from our witness.

The Cambodian Border

I have been arrested and persecuted many times, but the last time—two weeks ago with the border guards of Kampuchea (Cambodia)—was the worst. I was arrested at ten o'clock in the morning about one kilometer from the border. A police-woman made me take my clothes off to check if I was carrying anything "illegal" on me. They pushed me down and threatened me.

They knew about the workers going across the border, spreading this strange religion into their land. So they phoned the Vietnamese guards and complained, "Why do you allow this preacher in your country to come into ours?"

The guards questioned me, and then transferred me to the Binh Long district. They took away the 23 tracts called, "Is Jesus the Son of God?" They called the tracts "Bibles." They phoned the district police office and said that they found over 30 Bibles on me. During the night, they questioned me, "Why do you come here to this border zone?"

I told them that I didn't know it was a border. It did not have a stop sign.

They asked me why I had come. I told them I had brothers and sisters who were Christians and I wanted to visit them.

Throughout the night, ten district policemen continued to interrogate me. At about one o'clock in the morning, they spread a picture of Jesus and the tracts out on the table. They read them. All during this time, they were threatening me, yelling and shouting at me. The Lord reminded me of the verse, "I have given you the authority to trample under your feet the snake and scorpion." So, as I looked straight into the eyes of each man who was yelling at me, I silently prayed and bound them in the name of the Lord. One by one they left the

room. Thang, the only policeman who stayed there, told me
to follow him to a prison cell.

I said, "No, I will sit here. I will not stay in the prison even
one night, because I have committed no crime. So even if you
bring me to the prison, I will go back to Saigon and tell the
newspaper why you arrested me. You must tell the truth. I
believe that someday you will believe in Jesus also."

Then Thang took me to a temporary prison, a better room.
That night I prayed to the Lord, because the police confiscated my motorbike and my money. I prayed, "I don't want to
stay here even though they sentenced me to one to three
months. Tomorrow I will leave with my motorbike and my
money."

The next day, I was not fined any money. I was given back
my motorbike, because I had been arrested in the border
zone. This motorbike I use for mission work is heavy, not like
my own little one. I had never driven this heavier motorbike
before. The young worker who drove me had also been arrested, but he had escaped from the police.

In order to get out to the border office station that morning, I had to take the motorbike up and down a hill and go out
to the road. I am 54 years old. I had never driven a motorbike—not even a bicycle. Others would drive for me. I usually
took the bus, then walked to a tribe. I prayed and had to
pretend like I knew how to drive the motorbike.

At this time in the morning, more than 40 policemen had
come back to the station after their night-watch guard duty.
They stood there watching me with the motorbike. I tied my
bags up and prayed to the Lord, "God, now you must help me
to move this motorbike down and up the hill." I set the brake,
just like I knew how to use it. And just like somebody was
pushing behind me, the Lord did a miracle. I coasted it down
and pushed it up.

Now I was by myself, alone. How could I ride this motorbike
back? I prayed again, "Lord, how can I ride this?"

I stopped at a small hut along the road for something to drink. The girl there said, "Watch out for men on their motorbikes. They will kill you and take away your motorbike."

The Lord sent a man on a motorbike. The driver's face was kind. I prayed. I told him I would pay him to go back to his home and return to help me ride my motorbike. He agreed. He drove his motorbike back to his home and asked his wife to drive him back to me. She drove their motorbike back home, and he drove my motorbike and went with me.

Sitting behind him, I shared the gospel in his ear for two days. When we arrived at my village, I asked the brothers to pray for him to receive Jesus. He became a Christian.

I have many favorite Bible verses. These are two: Matthew 5:11, "Blessed are you when they revile and persecute you... for My sake," and 2 Timothy 2:12, "If we endure, we shall also reign with Him."

CHAPTER 17

A Grandmother's Bold Faith

If You Shave a Tiger's Hair

If you shave a tiger's hair, it will grow back again just like it was—with stripes. When the police arrested me for preaching the gospel, they hoped to destroy my faith. But when I was finally released, my faith—like the tiger's hair—had grown and my stripes were still there.

In 1989 I joined a house church in my village of Thanh Myloi in Thu Duc Province. Hundreds of people gathered at my home to hear the gospel. The police tried to stop us many times, but we refused. Finally in 1992, as we celebrated an Easter meeting with fellowship and food, the police surrounded my home and heard us. Then they pushed open the kitchen door and came in. They called me back to the kitchen, because the meeting was in the front of the house. The police repeated to me five times to stop meeting, but I kept on praying and continued despite their orders.

One day about 30 or 40 policemen surrounded my house. More than 30 Christians were in the meeting.

Mrs. Vo Thi Manh and her daughter, Nguyen Thi Ngoc My

145

The police looked into every face there, but focused on me and Brother Ba Tai.

"You are too strict on us," I told them.

One policeman furiously tried to kick me, swinging his leg hard, but missed in the air! He shouted, "I will kill you! I will shoot you!"

Near the end of the meeting, Ba Tai and his wife tried to leave the room, but the police wouldn't let them. They struggled as the police taunted them, "What are you doing? Do you want to steal something?"

The next day, many policemen came to my house to arrest me. I was 62 years old, and still had two daughters at home. They asked, "Why did you arrest my mom?"

The police warned, "If you shout, I also will arrest you too."

The men were very strong. Although I refused to go, they pulled me by the arm, threw me into the car, and drove away. I sat in the back between two policemen. It took 50 minutes to ride from my house to the prison. I felt very much at peace. If I had not believed in the Lord, I would be dead because of my sickness and because of my sin. So now I live and am willing to suffer for the Lord.

They brought me into a cell three meters wide by six meters long, which held about 19 ladies. The toilet was there. Inside I saw three ropes hanging from the beams in the roof where three women prisoners had hanged themselves. Everyone laid down sideways on the floor to sleep. I had to sleep without a blanket for two weeks until I got one. Many of the women had scabby skin.

The Spiritual Battle

The people in the room were very afraid. Many times they tried to rest but claimed to see the spirits of the women who had hanged themselves. I didn't see anything. The prisoners were afraid of the spirits and often the devil would threaten people while they were asleep. They got sick, terrified of the "ghosts."

One night as I was praying, a 30-year-old woman was sitting nearby, terrified. I was sitting by a hole near the door for air. The Holy Spirit guided me to go and pray for this woman because the devil was threatening her. As soon as I laid hands on her, the woman rose up and said, "Oh, the devil ran, he has run away."

I started praying for others who were sick. Many of them were healed. There was a woman about 48 years old who had been sentenced to three years. She was very skinny. I prayed for her and the Lord healed her sickness. She put on more weight and regained her health.

A girl, 19 years old, got itching things like scabies all over her body. I prayed for her one morning and she was healed.

One day when I shared the gospel, six of the women believed in Jesus. Many of them had stomach aches, headaches, or itchy skin. I also prayed for them, and their families no longer needed to send them medicine.

My family brought food to me every Sunday. After my arrest, I knew that many brothers and sisters and my pastor were praying for me, so I was greatly strengthened. I knew that Christians in other countries were praying for me. Even though we have different skin colors, in the Lord we are all one.

Inside the prison, we were given rice to eat. When you receive extra food from friends not in prison, you can share it with a friend. In the morning, we had to get up and roll up our straw mat. We were not allowed to sleep a long time.

I was the oldest woman in the room. They respected me, calling me "Auntie," "Grandma," or "Sister." I sang for them, but they couldn't learn the songs; they were distracted.

I received two letters from overseas. One was typed in Vietnamese. The police said, "Who are these people that you know? Foreigners?" I said I didn't know any foreigners, they just write to me.

I stayed in Thu Duc Prison for 11 months and a few days, never going outside my cell for exercise. One month before

the police transferred me to Chi Hoa Camp, a new prisoner built a small altar with ropes and brought some food to worship the spirits of the three who had hanged themselves.

On the day of my transfer to Chi Hoa Camp, I had a chance to say goodbye to my cell mates. I said to the two younger ones, "Auntie Hai (my nickname) will have to go to Chi Hoa Camp, but I will still pray for you that the Lord will soon release you. When you get out, remember the Lord and come to my house." I gave them my address, so they could visit me someday. Then I said goodbye. They cried a lot, hugging me and trying to pull me back. The police saw this. So when I went through the door, they scolded me.

The police took me to the other prison on a big U.S. Army truck. It was empty in the back. Five of us Christians were brought out together: Brother Nguyen Ba Tai, Brother Dung, Brother Long, Brother Minh, and me. We were all from the same house church. The men had been together in another cell. We were so happy to see one another again. We greeted each other with, "Hi Dung! Hi Minh! Hi Long!"

The truck was dirty. We all sat on the floor with our legs chained to a long metal bar. Brother Long, who had been coming to my house for church meetings, had only one leg. We sat there with one guard armed with a rifle.

The trip took 45 minutes. During this time, we encouraged one another. The men said to me,

"Oh, praise the Lord that we meet you again. Be strong."
Because the policeman was standing in the truck, we did not
discuss anything secret, but joyfully said, "Oh thank you, officer, for allowing us to meet again."

"Home" at Chi Hoa

We arrived at Chi Hoa and went through the big gate. This
would be my "home" for seven months. A guard put me in a
cell with more than 30 people for one day and night. The next
morning at eight o'clock, the police led me to a cell on the
third floor. I stayed there until the day they released me.

This tiny room was about three meters wide and three
meters long and had a toilet in it. We had only one hole in the
ceiling. My eyes weakened because of the darkness, and I
could not see even two meters away.

Feeling bad at this time, I asked the Lord to help me so I
could read my Bible again. The Word is my life, the life of my
soul. That time of isolation in the dark cell was hard on my
eyes. I can read the Bible today, but when I go out into the sun,
the bright daylight hurts my eyes.

There was another woman with me, a Catholic named Na.
She came from Dong Nai Province. Aged 52, she had a round
face, and was short and a little fat. She came to Chi Hoa ten
months before me and supposedly stayed there for five
months after I was released. She was arrested because she led
protests, accusing the government of corruption, like stealing
the property of the people and bribing. Many people had
joined her in the protests.

When I first stepped into this room, she complained to the
policeman saying, "I thought you would bring a young woman
to my cell so that I would have better company, but you bring
an older lady. I feel worse."

But after a couple of days, we began talking to each other
and became friends. In the beginning, she prayed alone in
a Catholic manner using the rosary. Eventually, we prayed
together a lot.

Inside the cell it was very hot, so we wore only underwear and short pants. Even though it was hot and dark inside the cell, I continued to pray, sing, and rely on the Lord.

There was a young man in the cell next door. I found a little hole where I could slip my hand over to him and he could touch my hand. Sometimes I gave my food to him because no one brought food to the prison for him. I also shared the gospel with him, and he accepted Christ.

A 36-year-old man who had been a robber in Cambodia was put in a room above me on the fourth floor. I talked to him through a hole in the ceiling. He had to lay down and place his ear near the hole to listen. I shared the gospel and he also believed in Christ.

Besides my ten children, I have 19 or 20 grandchildren. Many came to visit. Twice a week they allowed me to see them face-to-face through a fence. There is a hole in the fence where families could pass food. They would say, "Grandma, Grandma, what a surprise! Grandma is in prison!" The grandchildren could not understand why they had to stand behind a fence. Perhaps they also didn't know what a prison is.

My children would send me food once a week. Later on, the police no longer allowed the families to bring food. They were told, "Send money to buy a coupon."

One day they allowed me to go out two times to buy some things they sell inside the prison. I could never see the sky, even when I took coupons from the prison (money given by relatives) to buy some cooked fish and fruits.

On October 30, 1993, I was transferred by jeep to Vien Kiem Soat in the Thu Duc area for release. The police escorted me to my community in Thu Duc where I met my family and many others outside of my home.

Handing me a microphone, the police let me speak before hundreds of people in our community. "I was preaching. That's why the government arrested me," I said boldly. "I request that the government leave Christians alone and let us meet freely at home, so that we can pursue our faith."

Freely Ministering

In the Bible, I like the story of how Jesus shed His blood to save me. My favorite verse is, "Ask and it will be given to you; seek and you will find; knock and the door will be opened to you" (Matthew 7:7).

Just like shaving a tiger's hair doesn't do away with its stripes, so I am still a Christian. I still have meetings. At first there were only five meetings in my house; now there are more than a dozen.

CHAPTER 18

Pulling Down Strongholds

⚜

No Greater Joy

One of the most exciting, joyful times for me was when I was in prison. After serving the Lord, being in prison gave me much time to be quiet before Him.

For the first three months, I was confined to an isolation cell. During that time, I received a vision from God about what I should do after my release. I do not like serving the Lord according to tradition, like a wheel rolling over and over again; I like facing a challenge. The more I questioned the Lord about this new vision, the more He showed me about myself. I had to repent more and more. After a long time of repenting, the Lord started to encourage me.

In isolation I had many friends: rats, roaches, mosquitoes. The rats came into my very dirty room through a big hole, pushing away my rice bowl that I used to cover the hole. When I slept, I had to wrap the blanket around me so they wouldn't

Pastor Nguyen, teaching in a house church

153

disturb me. I heard all kinds of noises—laughing, crying, shouting, singing—all the noises from this hell.

Although I had prepared my mind to go to prison, I felt homesick and missed the church very much. I had no one to talk to but God. As I waited upon Him, He showed me that I would stay in prison a short time and would eventually serve Him in a place free of Communism.

Prayer was the best food to keep me strong. While I was in prison, the brothers and sisters outside were studying Scripture, praying, and pulling down evil strongholds. I prayed for the defeat of my enemies and believed God for a release of His power in all of this. I prayed for the church to have victory over the powers of darkness and for the Muslim world. I also prayed for the work of bringing Bibles to Vietnam.

Since I could not see the light of day, I only knew that it was day or night when I would hear peddlers selling their goods or the noise of many cars and motorbikes moving around. I longed for the times I was called out for questioning because this gave me a chance to breathe fresh air in the hall.

Phan Dang Luu

After three months in isolation, I was transferred to Phan Dang Luu Prison in the Binh Thanh district. One policeman from the Domestic Affairs Bureau, Captain Thang, was from South Vietnam. During the war, he went to the North. After the war, he came back and began working as a policeman of domestic affairs. He worked with me for three months.

Captain Thang wore the uniform of a domestic policeman complete with hat and medals. I had to sit very straight in front of him at a simple table. Usually there was a teapot and two cups on the table. He wrote down my answers on a piece of paper, and, whenever I wanted, I also took notes. Often he would get angry with me and stalk out of the room, returning a short time later to continue his questioning.

Captain Thang sometimes tried to talk nice and tempt me by saying, "I have the authority to release you." But when I wouldn't agree to his suggestions, he would threaten and mentally oppress me. He questioned me about house church groups and for information about the people in the official church. One day, he asked me what I thought about Bui Hoanh Thu, known to us as the "police pastor" in Hanoi.

I answered, "He is not a pastor."

Mr. Thang asked why.

"Because he does not preach from the Bible. He preaches Communism."

"Why don't you stay in the official church?" Thang demanded. "You split up and formed house churches."

"Spiritually, I didn't establish the house church," I responded, sipping slowly on my cup of tea. "God did."

"Where do you get the money to continue in this?"

"Oh, the children of God give generously to the work of God."

Thang lit a cigarette, took a deep puff and narrowed his eyes. "But we didn't permit you to ask for money from the people!"

I shrugged and casually set my cup down on the table. "It is true. I didn't ask them. They gave it to the Lord. They didn't give to me."

"Who are your workers? What are their names and ages?" he demanded, his voice rising.

"The workers that I have trained are so many that I cannot remember them all."

"You have not been ordained as a pastor yet, so why *are* you a pastor?" he shouted.

I nodded. "Yes, I have not been ordained. The people call me pastor and that means a shepherd of the flock."

The captain paused to scribble my response. "Do you have any relationship with other house churches?" he persisted.

I looked at him coolly. "Yes, all the other house churches are very good."

Thang stood, knocked his chair aside, and once again stormed out of the room.

I had written a paper about the persecution of Christians in Vietnam, which the police found in my home. They questioned me a long time about that paper. I did not know at the time that thousands of Christians around the world were writing letters about me to Vietnamese government officials.

In my writing about the history of the persecuted church, I had criticized the lack of religious freedom. During one of our questioning sessions, Captain Thang challenged me on this. "How could you dare to accuse the government of not giving freedom of religion?"

I leaned forward in my chair, my voice steady, "Because in this Communist country, there is no freedom of religion!"

He fidgeted with his package of cigarettes. "You accuse us like that, but there is no proof. Prove it."

"Very easy!" I shot back. "I am here and that's proof that there is no religious freedom."

The captain jumped to his feet and stomped outside. Regaining his composure, he returned a few moments later and continued, "Under the former regime of President Thieu Ky, there was no freedom of religion."

"You never lived under Thieu Ky's government, so you don't know that," I argued. "Under Ky's rule, if we wanted to build a church, we just built it. If we wanted to preach, we just preached. If we wanted to distribute tracts, we just gave them out. Nobody stopped us."

The captain kept to his government propaganda. "No. In Communist countries, all kinds of religions are present."

I smiled. "Yes, that's true. They are present, but they have become your tools. Even now, Captain Thang, you are serving Communism, but inside you do not find peace."

Captain Thang looked away and let his breath escape slowly as the truth of my words penetrated his crusty heart. "Yes, I didn't find peace." Then his eyes flashed. "But I then found that against Communism, there is no greater ideology in the world."

When I reminded the captain that Communism was collapsing in Russia, he once again stormed out of the room.

During the months of interrogation, the Lord taught me many things that I wanted to write down. I asked my wife to push some pencil lead into a banana and stuff used cigarette paper inside dried instant noodle bags. My wife also sent through five Bible pages from the Psalms and some of the books of the Gospels. She wrote me a letter telling me about the situation of the church outside and their prayers for me. Finally, she got caught, and the police would not allow her to bring me food for three months.

Since this was a political prison, many of the prisoners were men of great knowledge who hungered for magazines and news. They even wanted to read the Bible. When it was my turn to empty our basket of garbage at the end of the hall, a prisoner would call, "Nguyen, I will hand over some garbage." That was the way we circulated my Bible pages.

At night time, we would have music and entertainment. The guards allowed us to sing. Each prisoner would take turns singing. The others would sing the world's songs, then they would say, "Now your turn, Nguyen." So I would sing hymns.

Evangelizing in Chi Hoa

From Phan Dang Luu Camp, they transferred me to Chi Hoa, a huge transfer camp in Saigon for those who go to the labor camps in Vietnam. At Chi Hoa I was questioned only once by policemen who wanted to know if I knew any foreigners. "The foreigners are sending you chocolate, but because you are a prisoner, you are not allowed to receive it."

I was puzzled by this, but afterward my wife came to visit me and explained that the Christians in America sent me the chocolate.

At Chi Hoa, I was placed in a small room with sixty prisoners, and I got to share the gospel with all of them. In the beginning, there was not enough time to follow up the new converts. While sharing the gospel with someone, there were two lines of people lying down and one line of people walking back and forth on a path one foot wide made through the bodies. I would walk back and forth talking privately to the man walking near me, always under the watchful eye of the police and informers.

Although it was against the law to preach, I still shared the gospel and gathered my converts for teaching. Eventually, my wife sent me a very dark green mosquito net so that we could hide from the police under it. They could not see through it. We hung it using a piece of cloth with sticky rice. We put the rice on a big piece of cloth, then with a piece of wood behind it and a string we would stick it on the wall. Sometimes cloth like that could hold 80 pounds. Six or seven men could fit under the net. At night, we all went under the mosquito net. It was hot under the net, and we would sweat as we talked about God. But we were all happy talking about the Lord.

At night, some people would play chess or gamble. Some would sit around talking or telling stories, while others sang songs. Under the net, we had different groups of men visit. We acted out stories saying, "Now is the time for the movies." Some prisoners would act like Kung Fu or other characters. I would share about a Bible person like Daniel, Joseph, or Samson, and would act like that person in front of all 60 men. In my first two months at Chi Hoa, I had 12 strong new converts to Jesus.

Under Watchful Eyes

Eventually, I was transferred to the Tong Le Chan Camp. For three months I had to sleep on the wet floor. That is how I got rheumatism. In this labor camp there was no more free time as in Chi Hoa. This was a place where they punish you. They would bang on a tire rim to wake us up. We would walk to the area where we had to work. We walked two by two, just like the army, with the police in front and in back of us. They would give us a piece of land that we had to finish in that day.

At first the rheumatism in my knee was very painful. When I walked too much, it swelled. But I still had to go. Nearly every day, they changed the place where we worked. It could be ten kilometers, twenty kilometers, or one hundred meters away. We never knew until the next morning. We all had to go at the same speed. If one went slower, the police would ask that person if he wanted to escape. I had to use a stick to walk. The guards only showed sympathy if we gave them gifts. With the Communists, money is the best.

A friend, Brother Thang, the same name as the police captain, helped me. "Thang" means victorious. We had an opportunity to visit at his prison area and talk awhile. There he and I shared the gospel with others.

Every morning we would gather in the yard for roll call before going to the labor fields. In the afternoon, we would have to gather back there again and be counted to see if anyone was missing. Afterward, everyone would have one hour to take their bath. During this time, I would teach about Jesus.

We had to change locations all the time. I would sit in the yard or under a tree or by the side of the building. One time an informer threatened me, "Here it is prohibited to preach. You are preaching, so you will be put in an isolation cell."

"If because of preaching the gospel we have already come into prison, then going to an isolation cell doesn't mean anything. That is no threat," I replied.

A week later, the police put me in isolation. I didn't think it would be very terrible, but the cell was like going to a toilet—far worse than my cell in Saigon. It was a hole in the field with bars on top. During the day, I could see the sun. At night, I could see the stars. They chained one of my feet up on the wall and I sat like that all of the time. Later they gave me a handful of rice and some salt. I was there two weeks and thought that when I got out I would no longer teach and preach. When I was released from this cell, I drank a bowl of liquid sugar and cane milk. I was exhausted.

But I continued to teach. One night the police threatened to put me back into isolation. I shared my things with other brothers and prepared to go. But the next morning when the police called me up to the office, they wrote my release papers and let me go.

When Suffering Vanishes

If we think of Christ's love and the suffering He endured for us, then we feel our suffering vanish. I encourage anyone who is imprisoned to meditate on God's love and how Christ died for us. It greatly comforts me to know that the church around the world is praying for me; I am not alone. I want to give my deep appreciation to The Voice of the Martyrs. Through you, many brothers and sisters around the world know about my imprisonment and also that of the other Christians. We are comforted and encouraged. I desire to be a voice of the persecuted brothers and sisters, to speak up for them in the next generation.

CHAPTER 19

Confronting the Enemy

In the Pig Pen

The Lord has done many wonderful things for me. One time He saved me from getting arrested in a very unusual way. One night I was in a village preaching the gospel. The Lord warned a brother that the police were coming, so I picked up my things to hide. One man took my hand and pushed me into a place where the tribe keeps their pigs. A kerosene lamp hung outside the pig pen, but inside it was dark.

The police poured in, dogs barking all over the place. The moon was covered by clouds so it was very dark. When the police looked in the pig pen, they didn't see anything and left.

The Lord used many things such as this to show me that He is powerful and almighty. Although I grew up in a Christian family, Christianity was just a ritual to me. I often asked religious school officials about Jesus, but many did not know anything about Him, so I concluded that there was no God.

But one day the Lord started working in my life. My father was seriously sick and nearly died.

Brother "Vo"

161

He gathered all of us children around him and told us his last words. I was terrified because in our family there are only two men, my father and me. I had six older sisters and two younger sisters. My father's death would be a great problem because I would be the only man in the home, and I was still very young.

Despite our family's objections, my father insisted on inviting the Baptist pastor to pray for him. I can still remember it clearly. As the Christians next door used our motorcycle to bring the pastor, my father cried and rolled over in bed, groaning in pain. When the pastor arrived, he laid hands on my father and prayed. I stood there in disbelief.

As soon as the pastor finished his prayer, my father lay quietly. Curious, I went closer to see if he had died. My father was still alive, and from that day on he began to get better and regain his strength. That was the first miracle I witnessed.

I started thinking about God and about His power. *Perhaps there is a God*, I thought. I was not sure yet.

Later, when I was 14 years old, I came down with a fever and began to vomit blood. The hospital did not want to treat me because the nurses thought I was going to die; they were more concerned about making money than caring for people.

The hospital transferred me to my cousin's house. I continued to vomit and was unconscious. Through my cousin's prayer and care, the Lord healed me.

"There is something happening in your life," he told me later. "The morning you came, I had my motorbike out to go to a wedding feast. Something stopped me. I could not move forward. I thought the brake was stuck. When I checked again, nothing was wrong. I tried to push the motorbike forward again, but some unseen power was stopping me. So I turned the motorbike around and brought it back into my house."

My cousin said that when he put the motorbike inside the house, it moved freely. As soon as he parked the bike in its place, the car carrying me stopped in front of his door.

"If I had gone to the wedding feast," my cousin said, "I would have missed you and you would have died."

This caused me to think. I realized that there was an unseen being looking to my life, and with a broken heart, I received Jesus as my Savior. I cried and cried, not knowing why this was happening to me, only that the Lord was working in my heart. Eventually I became one of three leaders of the youth in church, leading the teenage choir.

In Search of a Wife

The Lord told me that my wife would be named Minh. In our local church there were two girls named Minh; one was much older than me and the other was preparing for marriage, so neither could be the one. Eventually, however, I met a girl named Minh in a house church. The first time we met, I did not know her name, but I felt that she was to be my future wife. I wrote to her that if she married a man who served the Lord, their life would have much suffering. This man could not guarantee her enough provisions, money, or family life, and he would regularly have to travel far away from home, and even be arrested, for the sake of Christ.

I asked her to pray hard about our relationship. If she couldn't agree to live under those conditions, we would need to move on in different directions. After praying, she agreed to continue our relationship for two years before we married.

Missions to the Tribal People

After our wedding, I began visiting the K'ho tribe to hold worship services. There I experienced many wonderful things with the power of the Lord pouring into those churches.

One time I went into a village to share the gospel. We met in a long thatch house that had two kerosene lamps on the floor to light the room. The people listened very attentively as I shared the Word with them until midnight. When I stopped, they didn't want to go home.

"I am very tired and want to rest," I explained.

Since our country collapsed in 1975, the tribal people had never seen any Vietnamese people come to visit them like this. They knew I had come a long way, so they let me rest.

I was so tired that I slept in a corner of the house while they waited. I awoke suddenly and looked at the clock. It was about 3:30 in the morning, and nearly a hundred people were waiting for me.

I quickly apologized, jumped up from the bamboo floor, and brushed my hair. I continued to share

Many tribal members in the highlands heard the gospel through Brother "Vo."

the Word with them until daylight. They went back home, and I moved on.

Opposition Begins

When I moved into another village, I met a preacher named Chan who was from a government-registered church. All the Christians were fearful of him. When he came into the village, he did not share God's Word but always asked the Christians to give him land so he could plant coffee.

The preacher asked, "Do you have official permission to preach the gospel here?"

"No, I don't," I replied. "But I have the Word of God that tells me I must come here to talk about Jesus."

"But before you came up here, did you ask the government?" he persisted.

"Jesus and the disciples, while they were going out preaching the gospel, did not announce to any government," I answered. "They didn't need permission."

"Then I will have to report you to the government," he said.

I opened the Bible to the preacher, showing him Isaiah 43:16–19. In these verses it says we cannot rely upon the power of the pagan government but must do a new thing. "Do not rely on the government to threaten me," I replied.

We didn't hear from him again. We moved on to another village and gathered about 20 workers.

One K'ho brother said that while he prayed, the Lord told him that I would be arrested. Another brother from Saigon who came up there to work said the Lord also gave him the same revelation; he ran 20 kilometers to tell me this.

I prayed and received great peace. "From here to the jungle train is 15 kilometers," I told the brothers. "So even if I moved out, I would still be caught. Everybody, go. I will continue to stay here."

While we were praying, one brother said, "At seven o'clock tonight, the police will come." I looked at my watch and saw it was five o'clock. I asked them to continue praying. Later the brother spoke again, "In 15 minutes the police will come."

I looked at my watch; it was a quarter to seven! I was the only one in the room with a watch. I said, "Truly this is a revelation from the Holy Spirit." I told the brothers to leave.

They took their things and quickly disappeared. I found myself alone in the room. Suddenly, a brother looked in and yelled, "Run!"

I picked up my bag. That's when one man pushed me into a place where the tribe keeps their pigs. Of course, the Lord protected me, and the police didn't see anything and left.

We slept in the village overnight. Early the next morning, we gathered the people in a house and I preached the gospel. I then told the church to pray. They prayed very loud and very long. I felt uneasy with this long prayer. If the police came back, it was now daylight, and the house was near the trail. I clapped my hands loudly to stop them, but they continued.

Once again, one brother said, "The police are coming."

As the church members scattered, I prepared my bag to leave. During that time, the police came and arrested a brother. The police knew I was there, so they waited a long time for me. Finally they took him to the district police station.

It was about ten o'clock in the morning. I went to the police office to visit this brother. I didn't think there was any reason that the police could arrest me because there was no evidence.

A Man Named Bac

I was questioned at the station by the police. "Who are you looking for?" they demanded.

"I am looking for Brother Linh."

"What is your name?" one officer demanded.

"My name is Vo."

"Did you come from Saigon?" he probed.

"Yes."

They immediately arrested me; I did not understand why.

"Brother Linh said you are the one who went with him," an officer lied.

"I did not come with Brother Linh," I protested.

"You are a liar!" another officer barked. "You came up here with four men. Your friend told us everything. If you do not cooperate, you will be arrested and given a long sentence."

The officers questioned me until seven o'clock at night. Finally, they wrote an order to arrest me and pushed me into a cell. A line of toilets was nearby. The cell was smelly and so dark that I could not see my hands. Another man was inside, but I couldn't see his face.

"Are you named Bac?" I asked.

A voice in the dark answered, "Why do you know my name?"

"Because I just heard the police say, 'Bac, I give you another man.' I have a piece of bread here. Sit up and eat."

"You eat it," the voice shot back. "Don't make a show, otherwise I will eat it all."

Later on I shared the bread, thanking the Lord before we ate. I was afraid that the police might use this man to beat me. While we ate, I shared about Jesus. I could hear him crying.

"Do you want to receive Jesus?" I asked finally.

Instead of answering, he cried out loud. I didn't know why this man was so quick to cry, but I decided not to ask him. I just prayed for him to receive Jesus that night. I also prayed that we would have a peaceful sleep. Then I laid down.

My head hit the wall. I moved to touch and see how wide the room was. I found out that I could not lie straight. The room was only a meter and a half square. Bac, who was shorter, sat beside me. Since the room was filled with mosquitoes, I used my raincoat to cover him. I fell asleep in another hour.

Later in the daylight, I was shocked by his face. His hair was long and he had a very wicked face. He had just been transferred here from the North. He had knifed a policeman who dared to question him about a case. The officer nearly died.

If I had come here in the daytime, I thought, *I don't know if I would have dared to witness to him. It was good the Lord allowed me to be brought here at night so I couldn't see his face.*

I asked him why he had cried last night.

"Yesterday at lunch time," he explained, "I said to myself that if there is a Jesus, who I had heard about in the North, then send someone to speak to me about Jesus. This was just something I spoke out, accidentally. I didn't think that a man like you would come into my room. The first thing you shared was about Jesus. So I know there is a Jesus."

I was there three nights and four days. During that time, I tried to teach the man about Jesus, but he had been confined in the tiny cell so long that he could not concentrate.

Finally, the police released me and instructed me to leave the area within four hours. On my way home to Saigon, I joyfully took the opportunity to visit a church in another village.

Border Crossing

One time I crossed the border into Cambodia with a tribal worker, Brother Nu Hau, to bring Bibles back to Vietnam. We were arrested by border police. They checked in the hem of my clothes and opened my wallet. Inside were addresses of contacts who would show me the way to Phnom Penh. I prayed.

The policemen said, "Oh, this is an address in Bangkok." I thanked the Lord for this miracle, because under this address was clearly written "Phnom Penh." These guards would know very clearly the different addresses, but they had "misread" it.

They pushed me into a room with Brother Nu Hau, who was lying on a bench with his arms handcuffed under the bench, embracing it. The officer tried to put a small metal shackle around my legs, but the shackle was too tight and very painful. He kept pushing. Another policeman pushed an iron bar through both ring collars on my feet. Unable to move, I lay there one day and night. I could only move my feet along the bar and spread them apart.

The police questioned me for hours, but the Lord also had His very wonderful way of deliverance. They found no trace of the Bibles and concluded that we had crossed the border only to buy and sell motorbikes. Under God's protection, the Lord delivered us out of this place.

Witch Doctors Set Free

On another occasion I came to Dong That to teach the Word. A man from Binh Ninh, ten kilometers away, heard that I was conducting Bible training and came to listen. He was vice chairman of the community and his wife was a witch doctor. He drank a lot of her potions and was demon possessed.

While I was teaching, this young man walked into the village and fell down shaking with his mouth full of water. The people with him were terrified. They picked him up to take him to the hospital, but as soon as he left, he became normal.

He tried once more to come to our meeting but fell down again, shaking, and the people took him out so he would become normal again. He tried a third time to enter this area and the same thing happened.

I prayed for him, and he received deliverance from the Lord. Later, I went to his village. The chief of the village supported me very much in sharing the gospel. Although he was not yet a believer, the chief was afraid of idol worship.

I had asked Brother Phuc from Dong That to go with me. The village of Binh Ninh was full of idols and witch doctors. In every house there was an altar about one meter square covered with relics of worship such as the teeth of a wild boar.

The villagers welcomed us. I entered the house of a witch doctor and as I laid hands on her and prayed, she started to cry and shake. Soon she was delivered and received Jesus.

I went to all five of the witch doctors' houses, and they also experienced deliverance and received Jesus. Afterwards they got up and took all their idols and altars to the yard and burned them. The chief also received Christ and encouraged the people to listen as I shared the gospel with them.

"Did you see how God delivered all these witch doctors?" I asked the villagers.

They replied, "Yes, we saw."

"Then is the power of God greater than the power of idols?"

They answered, "Yes."

Then I asked them, "Why don't you believe in Jesus?"

They answered, "You only prayed for the witch doctors. You must also pray for the woman who is the magician in this area. Only when she accepts Jesus will we make a decision. Who can save us from the wicked things of her magic?"

The people said that witch doctors were nothing compared to this woman of magic. They said they dare not touch her because even when many policemen came to deal with her, their families got sick and some of their children died.

I gathered the believers and prayed for faith, courage, and boldness. The Lord told me, "You do not have to ask, because I have given faith to you already. You just go and do it."

I stepped inside the room of this magician. She had a great big house with Chinese red tile on the floor, a tile roof, and wooden walls. I found her sitting in a corner.

"In the name of Jesus, look at me," I commanded.

She looked up.

We stared at one another a very long time. Then I moved closer to her and sat down. "Are you happy?" I asked.

She shook her head no.

"Do you want to be happy?"

She didn't answer.

I reached out and drew her by the hand into the middle of the room and started to pray. "Jesus, may You cover me with Your precious blood."

She screamed and dropped to the floor, using her hands as if to protect herself from the prayer. Then she rose up, screaming long and loud. All of my hair stood up. I had never heard such screaming. It was so terrible, I cannot describe it.

The people around me said that she was calling her different spirits to come. I said once again, "In the name of Jesus, may Your precious blood cover me."

Immediately my hair no longer stood up and I was not afraid.

I prayed for this woman for an hour. People surrounded the house because of her screaming. It was like the warfare between the prophet Elijah and the prophets of Baal at Mount Carmel. I declared Jesus Christ victorious over Satan. Suddenly this magician woman kneeled in front of me, folded her hands together, and pointed them toward me in surrender.

I told the demons in the woman, "You don't have to bow. You have to get out of this woman."

She collapsed backward and was silent. I prayed for the Lord's strength to restore her. We pulled down all the pagan altars, brought them out into the yard, and burned them. Then this woman prayed and received Jesus into her heart.

It was just like the wall in Jericho had collapsed. Everyone surrounded us, wanting to receive Jesus because their own eyes had witnessed the warfare. They tried to pull me in every direction to come to their houses to pray for them. Since it was already six o'clock in the evening, I told the people to gather in their homes, and I would stop and pray for each family.

This is the most beautiful picture I have seen in my life. In each house, I saw the whole family, often more than 20 people, all kneeling down, waiting to pray and receive Jesus into their hearts. After receiving Jesus, they all gave their altars and charms to be burned.

This went on until past ten o'clock. I had to go to each house, so it was very tiring. Throughout the village we could see the idols and charms burning and families watching. Christian workers sang victory songs. Today the entire village, about 300 adults and children, believes in Jesus.

Persecution Follows Victory

We gathered the workers in a woman's house for training. Her house was large and high up on poles. While we were in Bible training, two policemen came from the Binh Long district.

Usually the children would be riding buffaloes in the fields, and would run and tell us when they saw policemen in uniform. This time the police were in civilian clothes and sneaked in so quickly on motorbikes that we could not react in time.

The chief of the village ran over right away to meet with the policemen, asking them to come into his house for a drink so that the people would have time to escape. But the officers pushed him aside and stormed toward the ladder.

I was teaching and didn't know that the police were coming. They stood at the ladder, not allowing anyone to go up. So nobody inside the house realized that they were down below. A policeman made the chief of the village come, then pointed to our shoes on the ground. (When we go upstairs into the house, we leave our shoes downstairs.) There were more than 50 pairs of shoes.

Although I preached loudly, the police downstairs didn't hear anything. They only knew there were many people upstairs. They ordered the chief of the village to go up there with them while they arrested all of us.

The chief loved me and the people and refused. "I will not go up with you. I must work with the community police before I can work with you district police."

Leaving his comrade to guard the stairs with his rifle, the officer in charge jumped on his motorbike and rode back to the community police office. The remaining policeman soon became afraid and fled, giving the people a chance to warn us.

The brothers and sisters all prayed. We told them that in two weeks we would come again and continue the teaching.

I returned a week later with a woman evangelist and spoke in the morning. I felt tired, so another city worker stood up to continue the lesson. While I prayed, the Lord told me, "Go back to the kitchen."

I thought maybe the Lord wanted me to prepare the food or check on something. As I stepped down to the kitchen house, suddenly police surrounded the rooms where we were teaching, demanding, "Open the door." When the people refused, the police began kicking the door open. Meanwhile, the Christians were hiding all of their Bibles. When the police broke in, they angrily beat up all the brothers inside. The Christians quickly led me to a rice field and asked me to sit down. Since the field was very large, nobody could see me.

Everything was in chaos when I returned from the rice field. The police, joined by the village soldiers, had arrested all 18 members in the class, forcing them to strip to their underwear. Tying their wrists with electric wire used for hanging clothes, the officers had marched them single file about two kilometers to the police station. The 20 armed men had stolen the villagers' money from the house and had also taken my motorbike, Bibles, and bags.

When I saw what had happened, I asked the Lord, "Should I go back home or go to the authorities to deal with this?"

The Lord told me, "Go to the police."

"Lord, I am willing to go, but my daughter is only one month old and if I am arrested now, it will be very difficult for my wife and my little child."

But God encouraged me to go nevertheless. The power to open and close doors is within God's hands, He said, not with the governments of this world. This understanding gave me much faith, and I walked boldly toward the police office. The villagers around me cried, "They have beaten the S'tieng brothers a lot now. If you go to the police, they will beat you even more." But I went anyway.

I hadn't had anything to drink, and I was very tired. I stopped to get a soft drink so that when I arrived at the police station I could speak clearly. Otherwise, the police might think I was afraid. As I stepped into the refreshment booth, I saw four men sitting there drinking. They asked if I was called Vo.

I said yes.

"The police are looking for you," they said.

"Is that so? How do you know?"

"Your work, everybody knows about it," they shrugged.

I knew that there might be informers inside the villages. I said, "The reason I am going to the authorities is to help release these 18 people to go back to their homes."

However, as I stepped into the police station, I was arrested.

Winning the Argument

On another occasion I was arrested after visiting a village near Binh Lanh. At the police station, I sat down, crossing my legs. The police slapped my leg over to the floor, and said, "You don't sit that way in a police station." Then the policeman threatened me by going to another office to get his gun.

I told him, "Don't threaten me. You can shoot me if you want, but don't threaten me."

They grabbed my Bible, opened it, took out a picture of my wife and children. "It looks like you have a happy family," he sneered. "Why would you leave them down South to be away from them so long in the North, especially if we throw you in prison?" He waived his gun in the air. "You will be here a very long time. You are stupid for leaving your family behind."

I challenged the policeman, "You're an officer from the North, and when you came down to fight in South Vietnam, you didn't bring your wife down with you. Did you? You left her in the North, so you could fight. You and I are both fighting for our ideals.

"My ideal has been tested for 2,000 years, and now all over the world there are millions of believers, still fighting for this ideal. But your ideal has collapsed in Russia already."

He opened his eyes wide. Everybody knows this fact. Then he was silent. He left the room to phone the district police.

Soon about five policemen arrived in a jeep. One officer threw a Bible on the table and glared at me accusingly. "This Bible has been illegally printed in Vietnam. It is newly printed because the paper and the ink still smell fresh."

Another chimed in. "You are an educated man," he cursed. "You know the sentence for illegal printing. You have to tell us where you received this book and where you printed it."

I replied coolly, "Many of these books are sold in the old bookstores in Saigon."

The officer slammed his fist on the table and yelled, "Don't lie! How could government bookstores sell all these Bibles?"

I remained calm. "Around the city, many old bookstores sell all kinds of these books. So if you don't believe me, just take me back to the city. I will buy a lot of these books for you."

The police changed their attack. "You have been staying in a tribal village for three days, but you didn't register. If you were not doing illegal activities, why didn't you register? You must be doing something shady."

I stiffened. "In Saigon, I can go to my friend's house and stay there for three or four days. I do not need to register. I have lived in my wife's house for many years with no need for registration."

Once again the officer slammed the table, enraged. "Saigon is different! Here it is different!"

I quickly countered. "So you admit that the government in the city is different from the government in the tribes. But if the government is the same, then the law must be the same."

The police growled in frustration. "You must confess to me that you are doing illegal things."

"If I am doing something illegal, it is by accident," I replied.

"If we are speaking about the law," he huffed, "there's no word like 'accident.'"

Another district officer chimed in, "But you broke the law."

I turned and looked at him squarely. "Then why did you come to discuss things here? You have written a report of my arrest, but didn't write that you took away my motorbike. This means you meant to steal it! You violated the law of the cities."

The officer turned pale. He called the community police over and scolded them. "Why do you keep this man?" he demanded. "You didn't write a report about the motorbike?"

The policeman admitted this was true. The district officer was so angry he stomped out to his car. The chief and the rest of the district men left also. The community officer was very ashamed because he had been scolded before the high ranking officer. He apologized and released me.

Under Suspicion

Six months later, I returned to Binh Lanh. I had a woman evangelist on the back of the motorbike riding in front of two big bags full of Bibles.

When we stopped at a small restaurant in the bush, a Vietnamese came up and shook my hand. I was very surprised to see a Vietnamese in this tribal area. He acted very strange. "Why are we shaking hands like this?" I asked cautiously.

"Don't you remember who I am?"

"No, I don't remember you."

He said, "I am the policeman who questioned you. I have been transferred to the district police in Binh Lanh."

I prayed under my breath as I shook his hand, "In the name of Jesus, I bind you."

The official asked, "You come back from Saigon? What are you bringing here?"

As I continued praying in the name of Jesus, the officer became very soft and simply asked about my family. He said, "If you are going back to Saigon, it's already dark. I'll give you the address of my home so that you can go there directly."

I replied, still shaking his hand, "Okay. I can stop by your house if I have a chance."

We released hands and he left. I wondered whether I should turn around and leave or go into the restaurant to eat. If I turned back right away, the people would be suspicious. I wondered what would happen if I went into the restaurant to eat and the police came back. The restaurant was only 500 meters from the district police station. The woman evangelist and I decided to bring all the luggage into the restaurant and pray that the Lord would cover us.

While we were eating, two other policemen came. They looked at us and walked over to the owner of the restaurant and asked, "Do you have any jungle meat?"

No restaurant in this area served jungle meat. The policemen obviously were after something other than food. As we ate, we prayed, "In the name of Jesus, we bind everything."

The policemen noticed that we had much luggage. They talked softly to one another and left. As soon as they disappeared, we dropped our chopsticks and left. We quickly loaded everything onto the motorbike and rode in the opposite direction from where we wanted to go. We turned onto another trail that led up to Binh Lanh again. After going around many times to make sure no policemen followed us, we sneaked to the village and continued our missionary work.

While we are teaching, the police may hide outside and watch. Sometimes they chase after us to arrest us. Many times we are called to the police station for interrogation. But generally, every time we meet with them, we each learn a personal lesson. So in order to escape from fear of being imprisoned, we go to prison. When we are required to meet with the police, then we meet with them. Once we are arrested and meet with them, we have no more fear.

The Lord has truly blessed me and my family. I am convinced that when we are obedient to the Lord's calling, He will give us peace and grace in any difficult situation. I praise God for the hundreds of people He has allowed me to lead to Him. He truly has made "a road in the wilderness" (Isaiah 43:19) in the hearts of these people. We continue down the road.

Standing Between Two Tigers

B Y NOW you have a taste of what the Christians in Vietnam are experiencing. They truly live between two tigers: Communism and Buddhism. No matter which way they turn, they face persecution, hostility, and deprivation. They understand why the Apostle Peter warns, "Be sober, be vigilant; because your adversary the devil walks about like a roaring lion, seeking whom he may devour" (1 Peter 5:8). He wants to defeat the young church in Vietnam, to destroy the faith of those who are willing to stand up to his terror.

In this book, you have witnessed how these men and women have remained faithful to Christ. You have seen them face down the snarls of Satan's attack. These faithful endure great hardship, both personally and as a church body. In Nha Trang, the Bible school was closed, and now the government uses the seminary to teach politics. All the buildings, printing shops, and machinery were confiscated. In South Vietnam, the government concluded that all pastors belonged to the CIA. Officers arrested all the army chaplains and sent them to re-education camps. The government also arrested pastors in the provinces, such as Dieu Huynk, Eng Ai, and Pastor Vit. They were never seen again. Other pastors, desiring to win the hearts of the government, capitulated and now work as spies within the churches. These men confuse the flock and create even more danger for those who spread God's good news.

But the lives of the faithful show that while the tiger may roar, he may not defeat the church of Christ, which marches on bravely, aware of the danger all around yet trusting in an omnipotent God and, as a result, seeing miracles happen. Although they must disguise themselves, sneak into villages at night, and endure loneliness and cruelty, they keep bringing God's message of love to the cities, in rural areas, and in the villages. They are what Peter wrote about: "Resist him, steadfast in the faith, knowing that the same sufferings are experienced by your brotherhood in the world. But may the God of all grace, who called us to His eternal glory by Christ Jesus, after you have suffered a while, perfect, establish, strengthen, and settle you" (1 Peter 5:9,10). These brothers and sisters in Christ have staked their lives on God's Word and its promises.

Our One Hope

Praise the Lord that right now He is building up the fallen wall of old and is establishing a foundation that cannot be torn down. God is preparing the road for His people to live in joy.

As Isaiah writes, "Those from among you shall build the old waste places; you shall raise up the foundations of many generations; and you shall be called the Repairer of the Breach, the Restorer of Streets to Dwell In" (Isaiah 58:12).

Let's help them build up the walls through prayer. We can stand with them in one mind and heart to bring light to a dark world. We can encourage them to face the tigers and defeat Satan's plans, and we can watch God's glory shine through their examples. We can also pray for Vietnam that the government officials will see the light of Christ in their lives.

Perhaps the stories of these men and women have encouraged you to call upon God to defeat the "tigers" in your life, to serve as a witness for Him in your neighborhood, and to build up the persecuted church around the world. I encourage you to prayerfully consider what God would have you do. Make the cause of the Vietnamese Christians your cause. Stand against Satan and his evil designs. And see the change that results from your God-given faith and courage.

About the Author

TOM WHITE has been assisting persecuted Christians in restricted nations for over twenty years. As USA Director of The Voice of the Martyrs, Inc., founded by Romanian Pastor Richard Wurmbrand, Tom travels, speaks, and organizes mission projects in over one hundred countries coordinating aid for those who suffer for their faith in Christ.

In the 1970s, Tom made repeated trips over Cuba dropping thousands of gospels and Bible portions into the ocean currents and through the air corridor's of Castro's island. This was in response to the destruction of 100,000 Bibles in sugar mills. In May 1979, his private plane crashed on a Cuban highway due to extreme weather conditions. Brutal treatment from the secret police, refrigerated cells, months of solitary confinement, and a 24-year prison sentence were to follow.

During his imprisonment at Combinado del Este Prison, Tom, fluent in Spanish, experienced firsthand the plight of the suffering church. After many prayers, letters, appeals from Mother Teresa, U.S. Congressmen, and Christians around the world, he was released on October 27, 1980.

An author of three books about risking faith in a hostile world, he lives in Oklahoma with his wife, Ofelia, and two children.

Working with our international directors through a network of VOM offices, Mr. White continues to reach out to Communist and Muslim countries, and other highly restricted areas. VOM publishes a monthly newsletter giving updates on the persecuted Body of Christ around the world.

Other Materials from
The Voice of the Martyrs

TITLE	COST
God's Missiles Over Cuba, by Tom White	$5.00
The Spiritual Battle for Cuba, by Tom White	$4.00
A Window in Time, by Tom White	$5.00
Tortured for Christ, by Pastor Richard Wurmbrand	$3.00
In God's Underground, by Pastor Richard Wurmbrand	$7.00
The Oracles of God, by Pastor Richard Wurmbrand	$7.00
By Their Blood, by James and Marti Hefley	$19.00
The Voice of the Martyrs Monthly newsletter on the persecuted church	*free*

In the U.S., to order books or to receive our free monthly newsletter
and resource catalog, call (800) 747-0085, or write to:

The Voice of the Martyrs, Inc.
P.O. Box 443
Bartlesville, OK 74005-0443

If you are in Canada, Australia, England, or New Zealand, contact:

The Voice of the Martyrs
P.O. Box 117
Port Credit
Mississauga, Ontario L5G 4L5
Canada

The Voice of the Martyrs
P.O. Box 598
Penrith NSW 2751
Australia

Release International
P.O. Box 19
Bromley BR2 9TZ
England

Jesus to the Communist World
P.O. Box 69-158
Glendene, Auckland 8
New Zealand